WORKING ANGER

Preventing and
Resolving Conflict
on the Job

Ronald T. Potter-Efron, M.S.W., Ph.D.

New Harbinger Publications, Inc.

Publisher's Note

This publication is designed to provide accurate and authoritative information in regard to the subject matter covered. It is sold with the understanding that the publisher is not engaged in rendering psychological, financial, legal, or other professional services. If expert assistance or counseling is needed, the services of a competent professional should be sought.

Distributed in the U.S.A. by Publishers Group West; in Canada by Raincoast Books; in Great Britain by Airlift Book Company, Ltd.; in South Africa by Real Books, Ltd.; in Australia by Boobook; and in New Zealand by Tandem Press.

Copyright © 1998 by Ronald T. Potter-Efron, M.S.W., Ph.D.
New Harbinger Publications, Inc.
5674 Shattuck Avenue
Oakland, CA 94609

Cover design by Blue Design.
Cover photograph by White/Packert/The Image Bank © 1998.
Edited by Carole Honeychurch.
Text design by Michele Waters.

Library of Congress Catalog Card Number: 98-66700
ISBN 1-57224-119-5 Paperback

Printed in the United States of America on recycled paper

New Harbinger Publications' Website address: www.newharbinger.com

First printing

To Christopher Ronald Keith, the newest member of my family

Contents

Acknowledgments

I wish to thank the editorial staff at New Harbinger, specifically Kristin Beck, Farrin Jacobs, and Carole Honeychurch, first for suggesting that I write this book, and secondly for polishing and improving the quality of the text. Working with them, as usual, has been a pleasant, cooperative, and informative experience.

I also want to thank Mark Umbreit for his positive vision of mediation and the conflict-resolution process. The concept of conflict resolution as a journey of both head and heart emerged from our discussions and has added both to the book and to my personal understanding of the world.

Preface

In *Care of the Soul* (1992), Thomas Moore speaks briefly about the importance of work and the workplace environment to the human soul and spirit. He offers several questions a potential employee might ask themselves about the workplace during a job interview (I've modified them a touch to fit a current setting):

- What is the spirit of this workplace?

- Would I be treated as a person here?

- Is there a feeling of community?

- Do people here love their work?

- Are there any moral problems in the actual work or workplace?

These questions hint at just how important work is. Beyond consuming forty to sixty (or more) hours a week, work serves as the second center of most people's lives, different than and just as critical to your health and happiness as home. And, just like home, the workplace may be a place of peace, safety, and trust, or a place of disharmony, fear, and mistrust. Although you won't find total happiness at work (see my section on the differences between work and home in the first chapter), you certainly *can* find either real satisfaction that makes your life better or the kind of misery that embitters both your work and home experiences.

The working hypothesis of this book is that people really do want to get along at work. Very few workers want or desire conflict. To the contrary, I've found that most people greatly prefer harmony to conflict, a sense of peace to feelings of anger, and less anger and conflict instead of more. After all, people come to the workplace to work—not fight. The ideal is to do your job and enjoy the working atmosphere as much as possible. Most people dislike conflict, especially excessive conflict that brings out the worst in everyone, leaving people drained of energy and disgruntled with life.

A certain amount of conflict at work is inevitable, given the stresses people work under and the realities of people with many varying wants, needs, and personal agendas. I deeply believe that a little anger and conflict, well-handled, builds trust and increases cooperation. People emerge from these conflicts with an improved sense of mutual effectiveness: "Hey, we did it. We figured out how to handle that situation pretty well. I guess we make a pretty good team."

But note those words "little" and "well-handled." While a little well-handled conflict enhances workplace relationships, either too much conflict or poorly handled conflict can be extremely disruptive. This is why the three central chapters of this book deal with preventing unneeded anger and conflict, reducing the intensity level of conflict, and achieving successful problem resolution. The idea is to be smart enough not to get into many disagreements, to minimize the damage when you do, to figure out how to resolve any disagreements as amicably and effectively as possible, and then to get back to the feeling of harmony that most people need.

The goal of this book is to help readers understand how to manage their anger and conflict at work. I approach this subject both from a technical perspective—"how to" methods—and from a broader philosophical perspective, by which I mean that each worker must look into their heart and mind to take responsibility for every one of their words and actions. Both approaches are important. No matter how pure one's heart, for instance, you still need to have good communication skills to handle conflict well. But, on the other hand, anger and conflict management is never a simple matter of teaching people a few rational communication tools. Something has to happen deep inside each person in a conflict that allows them to *use* those skills in the service of a more harmonious workplace. It's the combination of specific skills and a deep personal commitment to mutual cooperation that helps people work together in peace.

I use many examples of workers facing conflict in this book. Many of the examples are brief, a few extended. None refer to any one specific workplace or organization, but every one of them reflects a real concern I've dealt with in my practice. There's certainly no shortage of angry workers and even angry workplaces in the world. Fortunately, there are also many people doing all they can to reduce that level of anger both personally and within larger organizations.

How to Use This Book

If you are reading this book primarily for information, the best thing to do is simply to read it through from start to finish.

If you think you have a personal problem with your own anger or tendencies toward excessive anger at work (or, if people tell you that's the case), you may want to look through the questions in chapter 6 first. You'll find information in the chapter that will help you deal quickly with an immediate crisis. Think carefully about the questions that apply to you, and then read the rest of the book.

If you are interested in the technical aspects of improving interpersonal communication, the most essential chapters are the ones on prevention, reduction, and resolution of anger—chapters 2 through 4.

If you want to focus upon a more broad philosophical approach to anger and conflict, then read through the material on good faith conflict practices in the chapter on resolution (pages 71–103) as well as chapter 7, which explains the journey of head and heart.

If you are concerned about another worker's anger, or you're concerned about workplace violence, you'll want to pay special attention to chapter 5 but also to the chapter intended for angry workers (chapter 6).

For everyone reading the book, I suggest you take the time to do the occasional exercises you'll find threaded into the chapters. They can help you deal with some central aspects of anger and conflict management.

Who Should Read This Book?

- Anyone who has experienced trouble at work dealing with their own anger and frustrations

- People who have found themselves the target of someone else's anger or frustrations at work

- Supervisors and managers interested in helping their staff get along better and function more effectively

- Employee assistance personnel and others concerned with minimizing the need for disciplinary actions, suspensions, and employee terminations because of poorly handled conflict

- Those people most responsible for minimizing the risk of workplace violence

Too many people in American society dread going to work. All of the reasons for this reluctance cannot be addressed in this short book—nor can I offer solutions for everybody. But learning to eliminate the useless conflicts at work and how to resolve necessary ones will help many workers feel better about themselves and their work setting.

1

Three Goals: Prevent, Reduce, and Resolve

Another Bad Day at the Office

It should have been a good day at work for Sally. It was Friday, and the last big order of the week had been packed and shipped on schedule. Now it was just a matter of cleaning things up and getting ready for Monday. One hour until the beginning of a pleasant weekend.

Unfortunately, that last hour was a disaster. First, Sally's coworker, Bruce, made one of his usual tasteless jokes. Sally normally ignored them, but this time she snapped at him to grow up. Bruce took offense and called her a thin-lipped snob. Sally retaliated by telling Bruce that his work performance left a lot to be desired. About then their supervisor, Helen, rolled her eyes in a "there they go again" gesture and walked out of the room. Helen never knew what to do when people got mad at each other, so she tried to duck conflict as much as she could.

Sally and Bruce sniped away at each other for the rest of the day. They both went home mad. So much for a relaxed evening. Sally's whole weekend may be ruined if she can't get that argument out of her mind. And probably neither Bruce nor Sally are looking forward to Monday.

Was this fight necessary? Did it have to happen? Of course not! This kind of morale destroying argument is both destructive and preventable. Yet scenes like this are all too common in the workplace. It could be anyone—the two employees of a small desktop publishing company; the staff of a social service agency, church, or nursing home. It could be groups of workers at a large manufacturing plant. A small workplace or large, blue or white collar, it makes no difference. Time and energy get wasted in useless strife and bickering. The cost to the organization is lost productivity. The cost to employees is more personal—who wants to work in a place where the atmosphere has been poisoned with animosity, hostility, and anger?

This book speaks to the prevention and resolution of conflict at work. Of course, it's unrealistic to expect there to be zero conflict. That wouldn't even be desirable, since a certain amount of conflict is valuable—as long as that conflict is centered around the goal of improved work performance and is managed responsibly. My goal is to help you minimize useless arguing at work while you improve the way you handle necessary differences in philosophy and practice. The three most important ways for you and your coworkers to do so are by preventing useless anger and unnecessary conflict, reducing and containing conflicts that must be addressed, and by finding effective ways to resolve conflicts as quickly and fairly as possible.

A Closer Look at the Three Goals

- *Prevent*: To anticipate and deal with possible problematic situations before conflict actually takes place

- *Reduce*: To lessen the number, intensity, and duration of conflicts within an organization

- *Resolve*: To work out solutions to conflicts once they've developed

Some conflict is inevitable within any organization. As I'll discuss later, many conflicts center around perceived scarcities. While many scarcities are created artificially and could be avoided, others are very real. Working time, for instance, can only be divided so many ways. An hour spent on customer relations cannot be simultaneously used for product development. Time constraints create necessary conflicts that force individuals and organizations to determine priorities.

But conflicts can be damaging. They may divert large amounts of energy from the normal operations of the workplace. They may seem interminable, destroying group morale. At worst, they can lead to breakdown and breakup. First, the organization's structure breaks down, leading to workplace paralysis. Then the people within the organization leave, usually separating with great animosity.

What, then, must be done to keep conflict from tearing apart an organization?

Prevent Unnecessary Conflict

Anticipate problems that might arise and prevent conflicts before they even develop. For example, a company may decide they need to put in a new payroll accounting system. The last time they tried that they simply expected their staff to put the system in while continuing all their other duties. That was a huge mistake. The usual software installation glitches took forever to debug. Meanwhile, the staff was under tremendous pressure to get everything else done on time. The stress just about drove them crazy. They became less effective at both tasks. The only solution was to dump the new system. Hundreds of hours and thousands of dollars were wasted. This time the company knows what to expect. They plan to appoint one person to take charge of installation, setting aside or finding others to handle her routine duties.

There is another aspect to conflict prevention, though. Frankly, many conflicts are simply wastes of time and energy. These useless and harmful conflicts must be stopped. If not, both individuals and organizations suffer. Ways to prevent these destructive conflicts will be described in greater detail in chapter 2.

Reduce Conflict

The second way to handle conflict is to reduce the number, intensity, and duration of battles within the workplace. This method is particularly valuable when there is a certain amount of inevitable tension between groups in an organization.

Let's use the Perfect Delivery Trucking Company for an example. For years, the job dispatchers and the drivers have been feuding. The root of the conflict is pretty basic. The dispatchers are responsible for setting the most efficient routes for the drivers. The trouble is, they sit in their offices while the drivers face the realities of detoured roads, unexpectedly heavy traffic, and clogged receiving docks. Gradually these two groups have become mortal enemies, looking at each other as awful and evil persons. The dispatchers call the drivers lazy and stupid. The drivers say that the dispatchers are naive and arrogant. It's gotten so bad that the dispatchers are deliberately giving especially nasty routes to the drivers at the end of the day, just to ensure that the drivers get back late. At the same time, the drivers are sabotaging the dispatchers by inventing fake problems to slow their traveling time down. Just about every radio exchange is filled with attacks, accusations, insults, and arguments.

This conflict has simply gotten out of control. Someone needs to insist that the drivers and dispatchers treat each other with respect. The goal must be to reduce the number of arguments and their intensity.

Conflict reduction methods will be described in chapter 3.

Conflict Resolution

The third method of conflict management is called conflict resolution. The goal here is to end a conflict, not just by telling people to quit fighting, but by coming up with a real solution that satisfies everyone. The terms associated with conflict resolution include negotiation, compromise, collaboration, and mediation.

Conflict resolution usually takes more time and energy than either conflict prevention or reduction. However, it's well worth the effort if a problem really can be settled rather than simply sidestepped for a little while.

Methods of conflict resolution will be described in chapter 4.

Distinguishing Between Conflict at Work and Home

Before moving on, it's important to gain a better understanding of workplace anger and conflict. Since most people probably think more about conflict at home than at work, I believe it's critical to recognize both the similarities and differences between workplace and home conflict.

Here is an example of how confusing conflict can become when people confuse the two situations.

Jolene: Managing Conflict at Work, Not Home

Jolene Adamson is an assistant manager for a furniture sales company. She's always considered herself pretty good at handling conflict, especially at home. Her style is to sit everyone down for a talk, get her kids and husband to share their feelings, and help them reconnect. Sometimes they resolve their problems, sometimes not, but her family always knows they are loved and cherished.

At work, though, Jolene is getting discouraged and frustrated. She's in charge of twenty salespersons who bicker endlessly.

"That's my sale."

"No, it's mine."

"I get that holiday off."

"No, it's my turn."

"The boss treats you special because you kiss ass."

"He does not. I do not."

On and on it goes, this ridiculous, morale destroying, petty fighting. But wasteful conflict can have serious implications. Last year Ralph and Liz, two senior employees, were fired for fighting right at the beginning of the Christmas rush. They'd been feuding for weeks. They'd been warned. But then they screamed at each other on the sales floor in front of customers. That was too much.

Jolene had tried talking with Liz and Ralph individually. She had even sat them down together to deal with their feelings. But nothing worked. Now she wonders if she's missing something. Why does her conflict management style work well at home but poorly at work?

Jolene is right. She is doing something wrong. The problem is that she doesn't know the differences between conflict management at work and home. So let's describe those differences now.

The Differences Between Conflict Management at Work and Home

Improved Productivity, Rather Than Shared Feelings

The "I" statement is the single most effective tool in the area of home conflict management. Traditionally it looks like this:

1. Say specifically what the other person did:
   "Last night you promised to come home at five o'clock and you actually got home at ten."

2. Say how you felt:
   "I felt hurt and angry."

3. Then say what you want:
   "I want you to call me when you are going to get home late."

"I" statements like this work well at home because the emotional atmosphere is absolutely critical. You don't come home to get more work accomplished. You come home to feel loved, appreciated, accepted. In other words, the main problem with conflict at home is that it endangers the climate of positive feelings that everyone wants and needs.

But that kind of emotions-oriented "I" statement isn't very effective in many work situations. Imagine Jolene saying this:

"Ralph, when you argue with Liz, I feel sad and annoyed. I'd really like you to get along with her."

Ralph's response (spoken or unspoken) is likely to be "Who cares?" Sure, he wants Jolene to feel good. Yes, it's always nicer to work in a happy setting. The bottom line, though, is that feeling good is a bonus at work rather than the necessity it is at home.

Conflict management at work almost always must be focused on efficient functioning rather than emotional care. That's because productive work is the central value of any workplace. While building and maintaining supportive relationships with other employees is very important, the bottom line is getting things done efficiently, effectively, and profitably.

This changes the very nature of an "I" statement. It's crucial components now become these:

1. Say specifically what the other person did:
   "Liz, you and Ralph spent half an hour arguing with each other yesterday."

2. Then note it's effect on your or the company's productivity:
   "That's one hour of wasted time that should have been used on inventory control."

3. Then say what you want:
   "I want you to quit using company time to argue. Any more

fighting between you two will count as break time."
Or: "Ralph, you've been shouting at Liz in front of customers. That's hurting our sales and ruining our reputation as a
friendly place to shop. I must insist you stop that, immediately."

The first major difference between home and work, then, is that
the home centers around positive emotions while work centers
around positive production.

Your Role, Not Necessarily You

At work there is more emphasis upon role, less on the whole
person. Sure, family members play out roles at home, such as "bread-
winner," "clown," and "taskmaster." But we are first of all whole
human beings at home. This means, for instance, that when sixtee-
n-year-old Jackie refuses to wash the dishes and angrily stomps
upstairs, her father Max will probably ask himself a series of questions like these: "I wonder what's bothering her so much? Is it really
the dishes? Or is she having trouble at school? Did she just have a
fight with her boyfriend? Are we going go through another round of
adolescent rebellion?" Dad might conclude that getting the dishes
done tonight is less important than finding out what's really going on.
But let's replay this scene at work, where Max is a lead worker
at a manufacturing plant. This time Jackie is a crew member who has
just refused her assignment. Max is likely to be much less interested
in Jackie the human being and more interested in Jackie the worker:
"Look, Jackie, I don't know what's bugging you, but I just gave
you an assignment. I'm going to have to write you up if you won't do
it." He might add, if he's the caring type, that maybe Jackie should go
talk with the Human Resources director if she's got a personal problem, but for now she'd better get to work.
Employee Assistance programs are very clear on this principle.
They are there to help workers with all of their problems—marital,
health, finance, and so on—but only as long as those problems are
affecting the worker's job performance. Max, for example, might be a
raging alcoholic, but it's none of the company's business unless his
drinking interferes with his job.
I don't mean to paint a black-and-white picture here. I'm not
saying that all companies are like heartless ogres who suck their
workers dry and spit them out (although, in all honesty, it's true that
some are). It's simply a bottom line issue. Companies do not hire

whole human beings. They hire workers to fill specific roles with their particular skills.

So what does this mean in terms of any two people getting along at work? Just this: *Any conflict that does not specifically and directly affect role performance will be ignored, while any conflict that does affect role performance will become a major focus of concern.* That's one reason some work areas feel like unchangeable battlefields. True, the people hate each other. Yes, if this were a family in counseling they'd drive their therapist into retirement. But, from the company's perspective, who cares as long as the job is getting done?

Okay, but then what does this mean to you, the reader, as you work alongside others at whatever you do? Exactly one thing: *Don't expect help from your company with your interpersonal conflicts unless you can describe the conflict as work related.* If, in the family, there are rules for everything ("Now, boys, you must speak nicely to each other"; "Share and share alike"; "No, no, no, you can't flush the turtle down the toilet"), most work places are more like a wild western movie ("Sonny, around here there's only two rules: Don't spit in another man's beer and keep your hands above the table at all times when you're playing poker"). There aren't nearly as many guidelines for appropriate behavior and you could get fired if you disregard those few that exist.

It's amazing how often a strong father figure shows up in those old westerns just in time to rescue the townsfolk (needy and desperate "children") from the villain. Too bad real life isn't like that very often. But it's not, at least in most workplaces. That means each worker is pretty much on his or her own regarding how to handle conflict and frustration. Each worker must take individual responsibility for handling those conflicts that fall outside the narrow range of role related stressors. We'll talk more about that soon in the section on individual responsibility.

Different Values, Priorities, and Needs

People get into conflict over many issues. Some conflicts are about money, others about power and control, still others about more abstract ideas such as religious preference. Over time, groups evolve sets of values and beliefs designed to help people handle conflicts well.

Perceived scarcity is one important cause of conflict. When people believe there isn't enough land for everyone, they may fight about land. If it seems that there isn't enough food, they may fight over food. People even fight for air (or at least the quality of it) as demonstrated by the ongoing battles over smoking on airplanes.

Please notice the single word "perceived." It is the *appearance* of scarcity that often leads to conflict, regardless of whether or not a real scarcity exists. If people believe a scarcity exists, then they act accordingly. In fact, many conflicts are resolved when the participants discover that there really isn't any scarcity to fight over.

Two perceived scarcities can lead to many unnecessary conflicts. One occurs when people believe there is a serious shortage of love that needs to be fought over. The other happens when people think there isn't enough respect for everyone. Although people certainly need both love and respect wherever they are, perceived lack of love is more often the cause of family conflict, while perceived lack of respect drives more workplace disputes.

As a mental health therapist, I've worked with many, many couples and families in counseling. True, these people fight over anything and everything: money, decision making, sex, child raising, curfews, school grades, getting the chores done, in-laws, booze and drugs, religion, and so on. But *the one single greatest perceived scarcity (and need) in families is love.* "Is there enough love to go around?" is the most important question a therapist working with a couple or family can ask.

With love comes loyalty. Home should be the place we can go when nobody else wants us. You cannot be "fired" from your family, because love is a primary relationship that centers on being and belonging rather than doing.

Sadly, too many children are raised in families where there doesn't seem to be enough love for everybody. Like starving baby birds, they try to kick their other siblings (or even one of the adults) out of the nest. If they eliminate their competition, they believe they'll finally get fed enough love to feel full and satisfied. These children often become adults who seek and need love and affection wherever they go. They may even come to their workplaces hoping that's where they'll find the love they need. Either they want everyone at work to become a loving family, or they hope to find their perfect mate at work. They are almost inevitably disappointed. Why? Because most work settings are not designed nor intended to provide intimacy or love.

Remember the key family question: Is there enough love to go around? Imagine asking that question at work. "Hey, everybody, do you think there's enough love to go around here in the plant (or office)?" "Look, pal," they'd probably answer. "You're looking for love in the wrong place." It's not so much that love is scarce at work. The main point is that its presence or absence is irrelevant. Finding love simply isn't part of the work agenda. If anything, love is considered a distraction, something messy that gets in the way of what's really important. That's why so many companies forbid fraternization and the development of "special" relationships.

Traditionally, the key perceived scarcities fought over at work are power, money, and status. Who has control, how much are they paid, and who gets the corner office with two windows? These issues certainly produce very real conflicts. However, *the main perceived scarcity at work is respect.* "Is there enough respect to go around?" is just as critical a question at work as "Is there enough love for everybody?" is in the family.

The odd thing about both love and respect is that they are artificially created scarcities. In theory, there ought to be more than enough of each, since neither is a "zero sum" commodity like office space. *Zero sum* means that there is only so much of that commodity available, so the more one person gets, the less is left for others. There may very well be only one corner office to be coveted by Mary, Drake, and Wilber. But why can't Mary fully respect Drake, Drake respect Wilber, and so on?

Conflicts can be negotiated far more easily once artificially created scarcities have been reduced or eliminated. In family counseling that most often means helping family members develop their ability to feel and express love. At work, that frequently means increasing the group commitment to feeling and demonstrating mutual respect.

Healthy Competition vs. Sibling Rivalry

Alice and Robert were looking for a new car when Dave, the salesman, convinced them to try out a particularly attractive convertible. The only problem was that Mel, another salesman, had just talked his customer into the same proposition. The two of them promptly got into a veritable wrestling match over the test-drive, a battle won by Dave with a splendid "snatch and run" move. Nobody interfered.

Now imagine that Dave and Mel were brothers. Can't you hear hurried footsteps and a loud voice saying, "Boys, boys, boys—cut that out right now. It's not nice to fight like that. Why don't you just take turns?"

Both families and workplaces must control the aggression of their own members against each other. If not, they'd soon be destroyed from within. At the same time, they have to allow some room for disagreement and conflict. If not, they'd be destroyed by inertia.

Most of the rules for managing conflict are identical in families and workplaces. For example, fair-fighting guidelines such as sticking to one issue at a time, sitting down and talking, focusing on the specific behavior you want to see, and remaining open to negotiation and compromise apply equally in both settings. (For more on fair fighting guidelines, see my book *Angry All the Time*, 1994.)

There is one area of significant difference, however. Many workplaces, especially those that are traditionally "masculine" in orientation, endorse the concept of "healthy competition" between employees. Colleagues are expected to work well together while simultaneously fighting for promotion, recognition, and reward. The goal in the workplace is to balance cooperation with rivalry. Conflict, then, is normal and expected in some work settings. Out and out war is not acceptable, of course. But as long as a disagreement is reasonably polite—as long as rivals fight fair—conflict is accepted and even promoted.

Most families realize that a certain amount of competition is inevitable between brothers and sisters. Who gets the last piece of cake? Who sits on Daddy's lap tonight? Who gets to sit in the front seat on that long drive to Grandma's? But most parents view such conflict as regrettable, something more to endure than to encourage. Parents hope their children will eventually grow out of this sibling rivalry as they realize that there is enough love to go around. In the meantime, they tell the kids to quiet down and take turns.

What about traditionally female-dominated work settings, such as secretarial pools or data entry centers? In my experience speaking with clients about such work environments, they seem to fall somewhere between typical families and "masculinized" workplaces in their attitudes toward competition. Open, obvious conflict usually is discouraged because, as the workers have remarked, "We all have to work together, so we'd better get along." Competition certainly exists, though, unfortunately it's often driven underground. The result is often that gossip, sniping, and sneak attacks must then substitute for more direct tactics.

Here's my position: *Competition is perfectly acceptable in the work setting as long as everyone knows the rules and as long as they apply equally for everyone.* You will learn later on how to avoid useless conflicts. But healthy (read "fair") competition is useful—not useless—conflict.

Workplace Conflict Resolution: Formal or Face-to-Face

Another significant difference between conflict at work and home is about size. Here's an example.

Milly, married to Joseph, is the mother of a three-year-old son and a six-year-old daughter. Milly's noticed lately that the kids have been fighting an awful lot. As she thinks about it, she realizes that the kids aren't the only ones who've been fighting: so have she and Joe. So, she reads a couple of books on conflict management, consults with Joe, and then announces at dinner a couple of new rules. For the kids: No yelling at the table, and no fighting over the TV—or off it goes for the rest of the day. For the adults: No fighting over money and no put-downs. Joe backs Milly up; the kids mutter a bit but obey. *Voila!* Problem resolved.

But what if Milly just happens to be the CEO of a business with perhaps ten thousand employees spread over eight plants in four cities? What if she's just realized that they, too, are fighting with each other way too much? Milly can hardly handle the situation over the dinner table. She's going to have to put a lot of people, paper, and policies into motion to effect change.

Leadership does matter, by the way. Businesses that make clear, for example, that harassment, intimidation, and violence are absolutely forbidden do have fewer problems with worker morale and safety issues than businesses where such behavior is ignored or implicitly encouraged.

Families usually only have two layers of authority: parents and children. Workplaces have many layers that aren't always clearly understood. Families can rely upon face-to-face contact while larger workplaces can't. Workplaces are notoriously slow to change, while families can change rapidly. All these contrasts mean that conflict must be handled differently at home and work.

There are many small businesses, of course, that operate a lot like families. Also, even large companies are divided into small work units, so that almost every worker has some more family-like interactions. Nevertheless, the guidelines for managing workplace conflict tend to be more formal and less flexible in workplaces. For instance, "mouthing off" to a superior is against the rules of most families and workplaces. Still, most parents expect and accept a little of that from their children, perhaps even an occasional "I hate you!" Children will seldom get "fired" for these offenses, although they may have to be removed from the home for severe offenses. On the other hand, no supervisor would be expected to tolerate such remarks. Minimally, the offender would get an oral warning, to be followed by written warnings, suspensions, and termination, if the behavior continued.

One implication of these differences is particularly important: *In order to manage conflict well, a worker must understand and be able to use both face-to-face and formal systems in the workplace.* Too many people rely upon only one or the other. It's not enough just to be able to sit down with somebody and have a heart to heart talk. It's equally insufficient only to be able to write wonderful memos. You have to be able to do both if you want best to protect your rights and minimize conflict.

How Getting Along at Home and Work Are Alike

So far, the emphasis has been upon the differences between conflict management at work and home. But there are important similarities that I'd like to mention briefly.

Habitual Methods of Dealing with Conflict at Work and Home

Some individuals are *anger and conflict avoiders*. These people feel very uncomfortable with conflict. They think disagreements are morally bad or dangerous. Conflict avoiders may ignore serious problems in the fervent hope they will just go away on their own. Meanwhile, *others seem attracted to conflict*. They often appear excessively aggressive to their family and colleagues. That's because they've never met a possible argument they didn't like.

Most people use the same approach to conflict at home and at work, although there are exceptions. It's very important, of course, for each person to understand their habitual patterns of conflict management and to modify them when needed. This means that conflict avoiders must learn how to confront problems more directly and that conflict attractors must learn how to say "no" to many disagreement opportunities. (See *Letting Go of Anger* [Potter-Efron, 1995] for detailed information on people's typical anger styles.)

Revealing People's Underlying Interests

In Fisher and Ury's best-selling book *Getting to Yes* (1991), the authors explain that people often get locked into apparently unnegotiable positions such as "I'm leaving work at exactly two-thirty every day" vs. "No, you must stay until three o'clock." Under each position, though, is an interest reflecting each person's core goals and values. Perhaps this time Alan, the early leaver, needs to get home to his kids so his wife can get to her late afternoon college classes. Terry, his boss, is mostly concerned that Alan fill in the next shift worker on what needs to get done. Both have reasonable interests. Now that they know these interests, they can start negotiating effectively. Alan, for instance, may propose to leave the next shift worker a written note explaining exactly what needs to get done. Terry may agree, especially if he decides that a written note could actually be more accurate than words hastily passed between two people going in opposite directions.

Three Major Principles Apply

- Too much conflict destroys morale

- Unresolved conflict destroys confidence

- Both conditions destroy effectiveness.

Too much conflict destroys morale. People become defensive, scared to turn their backs on each other. The heat of anger melts the emotional "glue" of good will, resulting in an "every man for himself" mentality. Within the family spouses start thinking about divorce while the kids count the days until they can escape the "madhouse" they call home. At work people head for their respective offices, cubicles, work spaces, or hidden corners, where they furtively look through the "Help Wanted" section of the newspaper. Everybody says they want peace, but nobody can figure out how to achieve it. Everybody wants to end the war, but no one is willing to drop their weapons.

Unresolved conflict destroys confidence. Maybe Mom, divorced three years ago, can't stand the thought of twelve-year-old Molly living with Dad, while Molly wants that more than anything in the world. The two of them keep talking but fail to find a solution. Mom starts thinking of herself as a lousy mother. Molly believes she'll never be happy. Both feel hopeless. Or perhaps management fails to decide which of two directions it could go. Should it expand or contract its accounting division? The bosses have hedged on this choice for over a year now. Meanwhile, the accounting division employees are feeling discouraged and depressed.

Too much conflict, too few solutions. Both conditions destroy effectiveness. People just can't function efficiently, at work or home, in either situation. Who has time to get things done when you're so busy fighting? Who has the energy to start projects, much less finish them, when unresolved conflicts have practically paralyzed everyone? Who knows how many chores, enterprises, and productive activities have been lost to excessive and unresolved conflicts?

Violence and Abusiveness

Conflict is natural and normal. There are many positive ways to handle conflicts, as you'll learn later in this book. There are also many negative ways to handle conflict, tactics virtually guaranteed to make the situation worse in the long run. Violence and abusiveness are examples of these negative approaches.

American society is becoming less and less tolerant of violence and abusiveness, both at home and in the workplace. Parents get reported regularly now for "whupping" their kids, which can be confusing for the parent who was raised in a corporal-punishment household. Meanwhile, employers are being sued for abusive behavior even though it may have been seen as acceptable in the past. The new philosophy is that all human beings must be treated with dignity. The sad reality is that many are not, both at work and home.

I will write more about the problems of violence and abusiveness in the workplace in chapter 5.

Varying Levels of Power Affect Conflict Management

Work has employers, managers, supervisors, and regular employees. Home has parents, older children, and younger children. Everyone is not equal.

Most models of conflict resolution assume equality between contestants. But a boss/employee or parent/child disagreement is not that equal. In both cases, one participant has far more power and control than the other.

In terms of conflict management, here are a few implications of this basic difference if you are the boss (at home or work):

1. Don't expect everybody to tell you directly and openly what they think, no matter how nice you think you are. People are afraid of power, no matter how wisely it's used.

2. You, as a boss, have a great deal to say about how conflict will be handled in your arena. You can set the tone for calm, rational discussions—or for heated, irrational arguments. Remember that you lead both by policy and by example.

3. Remember this old saying: "Power corrupts, and absolute power corrupts absolutely." You'll have to be very careful to use your power carefully.

What if you are the employee?

1. Be careful. Pick your battles with bosses wisely. You want to be known as a person your boss wants to listen to, not the one he or she dreads hearing yet another complaint from.

2. You do deserve respect. You have the right to protest being treated abusively or with contempt.

3. Remember to keep the focus on problems, not personalities. This is especially important when dealing with bosses, since you will always lose if a conflict becomes a personality fight.

Excessive workplace conflict is detrimental to individuals and to organizations. The next three chapters are devoted to dealing with the specifics of how to prevent, reduce, and resolve these conflicts.

2

Preventing Useless Anger and Harmful Conflict

Useless Conflict Wastes Time and Energy

"Look, I've got three kids at home, a million bills, and health problems. I don't have the energy to fight at work. I just want to get along with everybody."

Who do you think is saying this? An office assistant manager? A chef at the local diner? A salesperson? The CEO of a major corporation? The minister of your church? A man? A woman? The answer, of course, is that it might be any of these people. The truth is that most workers dislike conflict. They much prefer working together in harmony. The goal of most people is to get through each day with as little conflict as possible. A good day is a day without anger, fighting, bickering, or hassles. Fighting, even fighting over important matters, takes too much energy and leaves them feeling bad.

Many workers have one more basic gut feeling about conflict. They'd add that, in their opinion, most fights are about stupid, useless stuff that's basically a waste of time. Should we order Number

Two or Number Three pencils? Should we take our break just before or just after ten o'clock? Should or shouldn't the office clock have the company logo on it? Should Suzy Q. get a special nameplate for her desk that looks different from those of the rest of the staff? Who cares? What's the big deal? Why quarrel over such ridiculous issues?

The purpose of this chapter is to help people get along at work by teaching them to prevent as many useless, time-consuming, and energy-stealing conflicts as possible. The way to do so is by learning to recognize the signs of unnecessary conflict, and then to learn ways to keep from getting caught up in them.

Signs of Trouble in the Workplace

Some conflict is both necessary and inevitable in any work setting. But conflict is like a rich dessert—too much of it makes you sick. Furthermore, some conflict does more harm than good.

One of the best indicators of excessive workplace conflict is the presence of useless anger among one or more workers. Here are some of the signs of a work environment damaged by useless anger. These are modified from the booklet "Reducing Anger in the Workplace," by Ron Potter-Efron, published by First Things First (1996).

1. **Endless arguing, complaining, and grumbling.** People in these settings seem to spend most of their time complaining. Nobody has anything good to say to or about each other. There are frequent outbursts of anger and an ongoing negative atmosphere even in between these explosions. The anger is like a pot of water placed on a stove that only has two settings: high and simmer. It never completely quits bubbling away.

2. **Destructive criticism.** Gossip, put-downs, sarcastic remarks, nasty nicknames, and so on. Workers talking a lot about what's wrong with others and trying to convince people to take their side. "Wasn't Jodie stupid yesterday when she told me to switch headsets? She does dumb things like that all the time, don't you think?"

3. **Feelings of helplessness and frustration.** People who work in angry work environments often feel angry, helpless, and extremely frustrated. Nothing they do seems to matter much. They cannot find ways to improve the situation. Excessive conflict drains them of their hope, confidence, optimism, and joy. Going to work becomes an

ordeal to be endured for the sake of a paycheck rather than a place where you can feel good.

4. **Avoidance patterns.** Who wants to hang around with others when there is so much useless anger and harmful conflict? Pretty soon workers are staying in their offices a lot, preferring lonely isolation to hearing and participating in the nastiness. Suddenly that job in the Northwoods branch office seems quite attractive. So does working alone on projects even if they're supposed to be team efforts. And you might as well upgrade your résumé while you're at it. Surely somewhere out there must be a job with a better workplace atmosphere. Absenteeism and tardiness are two more signs that people are avoiding an angry workplace.

5. **Loud arguments, threats, and violence.** Yelling, cursing, "in your face" threats, pushing and shoving matches, hair pulling, fist fights. These are all indicators that anger and conflict are out of control. Now anger has graduated into aggression. The goal has become getting one's way no matter what.

These are some of the signs that there is too much anger and conflict within the organization. The results of these conditions are predictably grim: poor morale, lowered efficiency, decreased production, greater chance of injury, and workplace violence.

Characteristics of Damaging Conflict

The conflicts that make people feel the worst have four major characteristics. Harmful conflicts are repetitive, unresolvable, personality oriented, and about trivial concerns.

Harmful Conflicts Are Repetitive

Many couples have "we can do this in our sleep" arguments. These are conflicts that always cause bad feelings but never get resolved. The Smiths fight endlessly over money while the Joneses debate sex and the Andersons hassle over child discipline. Each partner knows exactly what the other will say. Their fights take on an "automatic" quality with both parties only half consciously playing out their roles. Still, each argument is painful and both partners would like them to end. But it seems that they just don't know how to quit arguing about this particular topic.

Repetitive, habitual conflict can build up in the workplace as well. Once again the issues get brought up frequently but are never resolved. Perhaps now the fights are about unfinished paperwork or getting done on time or what work should receive top priority. The specific issue really doesn't matter, though. What counts is that the fights go on and on, sometimes even after the original combatants have long since left the company. Melody used to argue with Jenelle about the quality of their graphic presentations. Now it's Helen and Herb loyally carrying on the tradition.

Repetitive, unending conflicts, whether at work or home, are exhausting. They're also a huge bore, about as interesting as watching a rerun of *The Honeymooners* for the two hundredth time. One reasonable goal, both for each individual and for the workplace as a whole, is to minimize these useless conflicts.

Harmful Conflicts Are Unresolvable

Dale and Evans, co-owners of Western-style clothing stores, are having a huge fight. Dale wants to take the company national. That's not enough for Evans, who wants nothing less than international expansion. The only trouble is that they own a grand total of two stores that are barely making a profit. Right now they're not even capable of expanding into the next town.

Meanwhile, at a nearby Western hat plant, JeanAnn and Hubert, foremen respectively of the day and night shifts, are battling over access to a small storage area. Both claim that their shift simply *must* put their finished merchandise in that space. Actually, though, the room is entirely too small for either of them. It doesn't matter which of them wins or loses because their problem will be just as bad either way. They'd do much better if they could put their heads together and come up with a plan to address their real shared problem, an overall lack of sufficient storage space.

These are just two examples of conflicts that are useless because no helpful solution is possible. While Dale and Evans are fighting over pipedreams, JeanAnn and Hubert have become distracted from their real problem.

Vagueness is what's characteristic of this kind of useless conflict: "Well, I can't tell you exactly what Hank's doing wrong, but I'm sure it's something. We just aren't getting the results out of marketing we expected." "Oh, sure! Those people over in sales are always looking for scapegoats. I'm not doing anything wrong at all. It's them. They should brush up on their sales techniques. They're just not very good salesmen." Notice that neither person can pinpoint a specific misbehavior of the other. Instead, they're throwing vague accusations at each other. This type of attack is worse than useless. It creates waves of bad feelings without generating change. Complaints rarely prove very helpful until specific, exact, and changeable problematic behavior can be identified.

Harmful Conflicts Are Personality Oriented

A few years ago, the major league baseball players union and the owners of the teams were trying to renegotiate their contract. Things weren't going very well and soon tempers flared. Names were called and accusations made. The owners said the players were greedy. The players called the owners shortsighted. Specific owners were publicly attacked. Certain union people were vilified by the owners. It got to the point where the newspapers reported one day that the representatives of the players and owners had refused to ride together to their meeting place. Eventually negotiations broke down and a damaging strike took place.

Workplace conflict becomes harmful when people lose track of the real issues and instead engage in personality attacks upon each other. Now the other person becomes the problem. People think that everything would be fine if only that jerk in the next office would be fired.

These sorts of personal attacks are called hostile personalization, and usually take two main forms: awfulizing and devilizing. *Awfulizing* refers to thinking and saying phrases like "She's terrible. I hate her. She ruins my entire day. As long as she's here nothing will ever go right." Awfulizers give away their power and control to the person they dislike. That person becomes an unmovable obstacle, a boulder solidly placed in the middle of the awfulizer's work path. Meanwhile, *devilizing* turns the other person into someone bad: "He's evil. Unethical. All he wants to do is take advantage of everyone here. You better watch out for him or he'll stab you in the back."

Personality attacks don't solve problems. They divert workers away from problem solving and toward gossip, taking sides, and defensiveness.

Harmful Conflicts Are about Trivial Concerns

Today's the fourth meeting of the Anderson Wood Products workplace violence prevention task force. So far, the meetings have revolved around one topic: Should children be allowed at the upcoming company picnic. After all, the chairperson points out, the presence of children increases the likelihood of accidents. But several members have kids they want to bring. They refuse to give in—and the chairperson won't back down.

Meanwhile, Penelope Mason, the representative from packaging, is fuming. "These idiots are wasting my time," she's thinking. "When, if ever, are they going to start discussing some serious problems, such as the tendency of some workers to show up hung over and mean?" In Penelope's opinion, that's what this task force is all about. She can't understand the reason for all this fuss about the picnic.

Harmful conflict takes place over trivial concerns. But what does trivial mean? Is the picnic issue serious or insignificant? Perhaps the most useful definition of *significant workplace conflict* is that *it is about something essential to the functioning of the organization*. Using that definition, Penelope is right. The task force is wasting its time on a relatively insignificant problem.

Conflict is physically and emotionally expensive. It takes a lot of time, thought, and energy. That's why it's important to try and restrict conflict episodes to important concerns about critical workplace issues.

What You Can Do Toward Prevention

The ideas presented in this section are designed for individuals rather than organizations. Nevertheless, I'm very aware that work groups, departments, factories, and even entire international corporations develop distinct atmospheres with regard to anger management and conflict resolution. You may be fortunate to labor in a workplace that emphasizes mutual support, respectful behavior, honest communication, and personal safety. Such organizations help their members minimize useless conflict and resolve necessary differences. On the other hand, you may be unlucky enough to work in an angry, hostile setting—the kind in which it seems that everybody is at war. It's more likely, though, that your particular workplace lies somewhere in between on this continuum: sometimes (but not always) you can count on the support of coworkers and management for help with anger and conflict.

Can any one person affect the nature of an entire organization? That depends, of course, upon the size of the organization and your particular role in it. You may or may not be in a position of authority in your workplace. No matter what your official job title, however, *every worker is in a position to influence others.* The way you handle your anger and conflict is bound to be noticed by your colleagues, especially those closest and most important to you. The decisions you make today, such as whether or not to get really upset about a missing piece of equipment, will be observed by everyone around you. Those decisions gradually impact your coworkers, much as tossing a rock into a pond creates ripples that nudge everyone in the water. How you handle that missing tool today, then, helps determine how your coworkers down the line will deal with their frustrations tomorrow.

Here are eight ways to help keep you from getting involved in useless anger and harmful conflicts.

- Take responsibility for your own anger.

- Make a personal commitment to calmness.

- Anticipate and intercept your anger and frustration.

- Realize you can say no to your anger.

- Pick your conflicts carefully.

- Accept difference.

- Praise instead of punish.

- Enlist support to create a compassionate workplace.

Take Responsibility for Your Own Anger

Hank Powers, a mold maker, gets angry a lot at work. He often feels like a yo-yo, pushed up and down by his employers and coworkers. First they tell him to begin design work on a new product. Then, they change their minds and order him to redesign an older one. That's when Hank begins to feel those familiar waves of disgust and rage. He often blows his top about then, yelling and cursing at anybody around. Hank's convinced that he's an innocent victim. He believes that his anger is justified, given what he's going through.

"They make me mad. It's all their fault."

"If it weren't for them everything would be okay around here."

"I can't help it if I yell. Anybody would in my situation."

These are the phrases Hank uses to keep from taking personal responsibility for his feelings and actions. They are the thoughts of someone unwilling to change on their own. Because of these ideas, Hank is almost guaranteed an unhappy and conflict-riddled work life.

The first and most important way to avoid unnecessary conflict is to take full responsibility for your feelings and actions. That means working from the principle that *you are the only one who is in charge of your emotions and behavior*. Nobody out there has the ability to make you mad or to force a conflict unless you give them that power. Certainly your coworkers can and will be bothersome on occasion. But that is an inevitable part of life. You have to learn how to put up with them just as they must learn how to deal with your sometimes annoying behaviors.

You must take personal responsibility for your thoughts, feelings, and actions. That is the only way you can remain in charge of your own life. Practically speaking, that means you believe and use the following phrases:

"I make me mad." Others may do things that bother you, but that's true only if you choose to be bothered. You must reserve the right to be the person who makes that choice.

"It's about me, not them." If those particular people who bother you weren't around, there'd probably be someone else.

"I *can* help it if I yell, scream, and so on." Nobody's got a gun to your head forcing you to act irrationally or disrespectfully. Your actions belong to you and you alone.

It takes courage to admit to ourselves that we are the primary architects of our fate when it's so tempting to blame others for our miseries. But taking that step is the single most important way people can avoid useless anger and harmful conflicts at work.

Make a Personal Commitment to Calmness

The teachers at John Henry Senior High have been feuding the entire school year. Sometimes they bicker over small stuff, like who gets which parking spaces. At other times they argue over bigger issues, such as whether certain classes qualify for college preparation credit. Morale is low. Absenteeism is high. Many teachers have become anxious, angry, and defensive.

Marnie Anderson, a tenth-grade history teacher, is an exception. Somehow she manages to stay calm in the midst of all this chaos. The rest of the staff at John Henry respect and admire Marnie for her patience. They wonder what her secret is, how she avoids getting caught up in their conflicts.

Here's the secret: Marnie learned a long time ago that if you go wading in a swamp you always get your shoes muddy. So, she decided to walk around as many of life's mud holes as she can. One way she does that is by making a conscious decision to stay out of useless conflicts. Sure, she easily could get involved in all those fights. But why? That would only make her as unhappy and upset as the rest of the faculty. Marnie treasures her calmness too much to give it up easily.

Calmness is a state of freedom from agitation in the face of possible provocation. But calmness is far more than the absence of anger and conflict. Calmness promotes an internal quiet, a sense of tranquillity or serenity. To stay calm in the midst of chaos is to give yourself a wonderful gift of inner peace.

Calmness is a choice. It doesn't just happen to people by accident. For many people, calmness begins with a decision like this: "I promise to stay calm at work for one whole day." That promise is a personal one, meant to help you stay calm regardless of what everybody else is doing. You are the primary beneficiary if you can make it and keep it, although your coworkers may also gain as they sense your new attitude.

Anticipate and Intercept Your Anger and Frustration

Thursdays are "get the week's orders out today even if that means working twelve hour shifts" time at the local mattress company. Every Thursday is a minicrisis at the plant, a breeding ground for anger and conflict.

Paul Jackson has worked at the mattress plant for six years. Just about every Thursday for the first five of those years, he'd wake up grouchy. "Today's gonna be awful," he'd think as he forced himself out of bed. Then he'd tick off in his mind all the bad things that would probably happen: His coworkers would show up late, someone in the front office would screw up the orders, he'd get out late and miss his favorite TV show again.

One morning, though, Paul had a thought. He realized that Thursdays were going to be Thursdays no matter what. He couldn't change the factory, but he could change himself. Paul decided he needed to prepare better for Thursdays so he wouldn't waste one day every week in futile frustration. He began a routine that includes getting to sleep earlier on Wednesday nights, taking the time on Thursday mornings to eat a good breakfast and talk with his family, reminding himself on the way to work that he can choose to stay calm, and thinking ahead about what he could do to keep busy during the inevitable daily work delays. He's also taping his TV show to lessen his anxiety about leaving on time.

Anticipation and preparation of possibly stressful events help you intercept your frustration. Notice, though, how important it is not to awfulize as you anticipate. You don't want to think about how bad things are going to be. That just increases your anxiety. Instead, you need to think in ways that help you stay calm and in control.

Realize You Can Say No to Your Anger

Imagine for a moment that all your colleagues at work are gathered around a pond. They've got their fishing poles in the water. *You* are the fish they're hoping to catch today. More correctly, they're trying to land your anger.

Some of those anglers have good bait designed especially with you in mind. Wilma, for instance, often uses envy: "Gee, I hate to tell you this, but the boss just gave Ben that new computer you had requested." Harry uses criticism: "You're doing that all wrong again. When are you gonna learn?" Doris makes nasty comments about your looks or clothes. Herm grumbles about "People who think they know everything just because they have some special training" while glancing in your direction.

These coworkers are trying to hook your anger. But all they can do is cast out their lines. It's you who has to decide whether or not to take their bait. Sure, you can grab it and start tugging. But watch out. Chances are you'll end up in somebody's frying pan. Or you can pass by those hooks, reminding yourself that "smart fish don't bite."

You might also want to ask yourself how often you go fishing and what bait you use. It's just as important for you not to try to hook others' anger as it is not to get hooked. That way everyone will be angry less often.

By the way, I'm not implying that your coworkers do nothing but sit around the office all day thinking of ways to upset you. But everyone occasionally will say or do things that could bother you if you let them. That's when their lines hit the water. That's when you have to decide what to do. If your goal, though, is to prevent useless anger and harmful conflict, then the choice is easy. Swim away.

Pick Your Conflicts Carefully

Conflicts take time and energy. Even when apparently settled they often leave residues of resentments that lead to more conflict later. Still, some battles are worth fighting. Not many, but some. The question is how to choose.

This question is particularly difficult if you are a "natural" battler. Maybe you grew up in a home where spirited debate was encouraged. Perhaps you believe that you should be aggressive at work because aggressive people get ahead. Or possibly you just like the feeling of combat. With an attitude like that, you'll have a tendency to fight too often and too hard.

It's also hard to select which battles to fight if you're an anger and conflict avoider. In that case, you'll probably fail to be assertive enough in certain situations because you've learned that getting into conflict is too scary or that saying what you want is bad.

So let's search for the golden mean that surely exists somewhere between getting into too few or too many conflicts. Here are six criteria that usually should be met to make a conflict at work worth engaging in:

1. It should be about something that directly and significantly affects or could reasonably be predicted to affect your areas of responsibility.

2. It should be about something that can actually be changed.

3. It should matter enough to you to be worth the time and energy it will consume.

4. There should be a reasonable chance that you can get the desired result or some compromise result that will partially meet your goals.

5. There should be little likelihood that choosing to engage in this conflict would endanger something even more important to you. For example, it wouldn't make sense to fight for a twenty-five-cents-an-hour raise today if it would jeopardize your chance for a three-dollar-an-hour promotion next month.

6. You should know the risks involved and be prepared for the worst possible results, up to and including getting fired. If the worst possible result is unacceptable (and more than extremely unlikely), you must ask yourself if you're willing to take that risk.

Not very many possible conflicts will pass all these criteria. If they don't, you should probably pass on it and save your energy for more important issues. But, if a situation does meet all these guidelines, then you probably should jump into action. Just remember, if you do decide to act, review the next couple chapters on how to reduce the level of tension and how to resolve conflicts.

Accept Difference

Many harmful conflicts develop simply because people cannot appreciate or accept difference. They confuse "You do that differently than me" with "You do it wrong."

One great human stylistic difference is between inductive and deductive thinkers. *Inductive thinkers* develop their ideas from the ground up, gathering lots of information before reaching any conclusions. Meanwhile, *deductive thinkers* try to develop their ideas not from specific pieces of information but from more general principles.

Another common stylistic difference lies between those who prefer more structure and those who need more independence to work at their best. When each group understands and accepts the other they use positive terms such as "firm" and "well-organized" for the structure preferers and "creative" and "flexible" for the independence preferers. But when difference is rejected, the terms become hostile: "rigid" and "uncreative"; "disorganized" and "chaotic."

Businesses work best when they include a mix of people with all these different ways of working. Imagine, for instance, a group of four craftspersons who've decided they want to start a shop to sell their wares. One person is inductive, another deductive. One is structured, another independent. Here's the kind of help each could provide:

The inductive thinker could gather information about where people go to buy crafts before the group decides where to place the store.

The deductive thinker could develop the company's mission statement and general business philosophy.

The structure preferer could take charge of the financial operations and other "must do" operations.

The independence preferer could help keep the focus upon creative work so that they don't get too caught up in money making.

This group will do well if they can accept each other's differences. If not, they will fail.

Praise Instead of Punish

Americans seem to live in a praise deficient society. Nowhere is this more true than in the workplace.

Bill Thompson is interviewing at Hello! Enterprises for a job as an Internet web page designer. He'd like to work there because Hello! is the most prestigious and high paying of the firms that have contacted him. All goes well until he meets the head of his department, Mel Nelson.

"Bill," says Mr. Nelson, "I want you to understand one thing about working for me. The only time you'll see me in your office is if you do something wrong. I don't give praise. I don't believe in it. Can you handle that?"

Apparently Mel is expecting an answer such as "Well, sure, Mr. Nelson. I'm tough. I'm independent. I don't need praise. No problem." He'd be surprised if Bill's response was "Thanks, Mr. Nelson, but no thanks. I'd be a fool to come to work at a place where I wouldn't get praise. I'm not a machine."

People need praise. Lots of it. Human beings are interdependent creatures who depend upon the positive evaluations of others to feel whole. True, you can survive without praise in the workplace. Many workers have to do just that. But too little praise and too much criticism is a sure formula for low morale, poor performance, and excessive conflict.

You may not be able to change the ratio of praise to criticism in your entire organization. However, you can take a look at your own habits in this area. One way to feel less anger and lessen the possibility for conflict is to look for things to appreciate and praise in others. By the way, praise is infectious. There's a good chance that, in the long run, the people you praise will start praising you more. But even if they don't, you will almost certainly have more work satisfaction as you learn how to praise more and criticize less.

Enlist Support to Create a Compassionate Workplace

The guidelines above are for individuals. They can be used regardless of the attitudes and actions of your coworkers. However, it's far easier to avoid useless anger and harmful conflicts when the majority of workers are committed to calmness.

Your choices are bound to influence others. You're setting an example every time you choose to stay calm instead of getting agitated, each time you remember that smart fish don't bite. But perhaps you can do a little more.

Melinda Borders works in the front office of a small manufacturing firm. She noticed a few months ago that the emotional climate in the office had become steadily worse over the past year. It's as if everyone there, including herself, were gradually getting drawn into a whirlpool of useless anger and harmful conflict. Melinda didn't want to keep working that way. So first she made a personal commitment to quit complaining or making sarcastic remarks. That took a while. Then she approached her colleagues. She told them what she was seeing and hearing every day: nasty remarks, excessive criticism, mutterings about leaving, and so on. She reminded them that only a year ago they had been much happier together. Then Melinda invited them to join her in a journey of the heart. That journey would take them to a place where once again they could enjoy each other. Her basic theme was simple and clear: "We've been at each other's throats, but we don't have to keep doing that. We can learn how to appreciate each other again."

Melinda didn't expect people to give her a standing ovation. What she got was a mixture of denial ("Conflict? What conflict?"), defensiveness ("She should just mind her own business"), justification ("She's right, but we can't help it. This is the way all businesses run, isn't it?"), and agreement ("She's right. We don't have to live this way"). Several coworkers committed to arguing less and cooperating more. Some noticeable change occurred immediately. More followed gradually as people discovered that working together harmoniously was a lot better than antagonistically.

The key is that Melinda invited her companions to change. She didn't order or insist. She simply offered them the chance to work together better. They accepted because it made sense to them. Why be unhappy because of excessive anger and conflict when you could work together in peace?

Positive Anger Prevention Through Self-Care

Anger prevention doesn't exist in a vacuum. After all, these are whole human beings who decide whether or not to get angry. The overall condition of these people helps determine how anger and conflict prone they may be. Good care and maintenance of your body is essential for anger and conflict prevention. People who feel well often have a better spirit than those whose bodies have been allowed to deteriorate. That better spirit, in turn, serves to buffer individuals against the daily annoyances that occur in the workplace.

Recovering alcoholics are often introduced to the acronym HALT as a predictor of relapse. H = hungry. A = angry. L = lonely. T = tired. The idea is that former drinkers are more likely to relapse when faced with any one of these conditions and far more likely to do so when two or more apply. I believe that HALT needs only one modification to be very useful in the area of anger and conflict prevention: Change the A = angry to A = anxious. Workers who find themselves hungry, anxious, lonely and/or tired are those most susceptible to unnecessary bouts of anger, irritability, and even violence.

The HALT concept can also be expanded beyond simply physical cues. Hungry, for example, does certainly apply to situations such as skipping lunch to get a job completed or forcing yourself to diet excessively to the point where your work efficiency is affected. But there are other kinds of hunger that also affect workers and make them more irritable. There's hunger for attention, the need to be seen and heard and to have one's existence as a real person acknowledged. There's hunger for affection, the desire to be cared for that makes going to work far more enjoyable because some of your coworkers are also friends. And there is hunger for affirmation, the pat on the back that tells you others can see you've done a good job. So, while good nutrition is essential for anger prevention, it's also important to feed your psychological hungers as well.

Anxiety and anger often reinforce each other. Both are part of the body's flight or fight reaction to perceived danger. Anxiety tends to develop when someone is gradually overwhelmed by fear-evoking concerns, even though each problem may be fairly low-level. The work scene, with its constant barrage of duties and time demands, is a perfect place to become anxious and then angry. The person who is stressed out at work, desperately running to get one more thing done and continually fearful of failure, may easily become quickly bothered by anyone who happens to be standing in their path. It's like Dagwood Bumstead dashing to his carpool in the morning and crashing into the mailman, except that the words exchanged would not fit into the cartoon balloon of a family newspaper.

Relaxation is an important anger prevention technique just because it lowers people's anxiety level. Relaxation, especially when learned well and practiced daily, lowers stress so effectively that they become far less prone to have their fight or flight response activated. Fewer alarm signals go off and that means that fewer opportunities for anger ever develop.

L is the third letter in HALT and it stands for loneliness. People may bring their outside loneliness issues into work, as when someone going through a relationship breakup becomes depressed and surly. The neediness of lonely workers can also become problematic if they try but fail to get their social needs met at work.

A more direct aspect of loneliness that applies in the workplace occurs when workers feel estranged from their colleagues. Workers who think, correctly or incorrectly, that they don't really belong or aren't fully accepted may be particularly vulnerable to angry and hostile feelings. "I want you to like me" becomes converted to "Why don't you like me?" and then to "Why are you so mean to me?" and finally to "I don't like you either." Since these disaffected workers feel little sense of loyalty to their coworkers they have fewer reasons to control their anger.

The T in HALT stands for tired, the constant state for all too many American workers trying to exist on two to three fewer hours sleep than they actually need. The result is low-grade fatigue that dulls the senses, lessens productivity, and heightens irritability. By the way, one way to lessen such tiredness, in addition to sleep, is with proper exercise. A consistent exercise program tends to energize and revitalize individuals, especially those whose careers keep them mostly deskbound.

Sometimes fatigue leads to burnout, that unhappy state when going to work not only is no longer enjoyable but almost intolerable. One of the signs of burnout is when fellow workers begin commenting on how their coworker, who used to be fun to be around, has now become a grouch. Burnout fatigue combines a "Who cares?" attitude with "Go away and leave me alone!"

Workers need to learn and practice long-term physical and mental health maintenance to combat negative HALT anger-producing symptoms. Physical hunger can be handled with regular meals and sensible nutrition. Emotional hunger calls for self-awareness, as well as the ability to balance work with social and psychological care. Relaxation greatly reduces anxiety, as does reasonable work loads and personal expectations. Workers who realize they are lonely might need to work on their social skills a little so they can make better friends. They may also consciously need to take more initiative to become less isolated at work. Finally, tiredness demands rest. People must take the time to rest, if only to improve the quality of their work and diminish the prospects of workplace aggression.

Being, Belonging, and Doing: Maintaining Balance

There's one more way to help prevent anger at work. That is to remember that work is an important part but only part of your life. Work is usually a person's "doing" focus—it's there that you make your main contribution to society, apart from taking care of your family (be it your own children or your extended family). Because work leads to feelings of competence or incompetence, it matters a great deal to most people.

But work isn't life and death. It's not the place you can get all your needs met, either. In particular, people can seldom fulfill their deepest yearnings for "being" and "belonging" at work. No matter how loudly work calls, it's critical to make time for self-discovery (the quest for being) and for relationships (honoring the need to belong). Those people who try to get these needs completely met through work are bound to be either severely disappointed or limited. To illustrate, the individual whose answer to the question "Who are you?" responds with "I am what I do" is certainly missing something in life. These "overdoers" are particularly vulnerable to workplace anger and conflict because their entire sense of being depends upon their work. Getting laid off, for instance, becomes much more than a financial problem and a cause for worry about the future. It can be a core-shaking experience for someone whose entire identity is in their work. When "I am something" is only correct when I'm working, then "I am nothing" becomes the motto of the former worker. Similarly, workers who attempt to get all their relationship needs met through work are excessively vulnerable to anger episodes since institutions such as workplaces can never really become the equivalent of families. These workers are prone to expect too much from their coworkers. They may seek love and emotional comfort inappropriately and then become jealous or enraged when those desires are not reciprocated.

Being, belonging, and doing are three legitimate needs that must be carefully and consciously balanced to achieve maximum satisfaction in life. People are simply happier when they can achieve this balance, just as they become at least vaguely dissatisfied when they cannot. Most critical to this discussion, though, is that frustration inevitably builds when people don't honor and balance these needs. Dissatisfaction builds both at work and at home, leading people to look for things that are going wrong. That negative perspective then makes workers believe that the people around them are defective, incompetent, useless, mean, and so on. But the real problem is not what others are thinking or doing. The actual problem resides in the heart and soul of the worker whose life is out of balance.

Nor can all one's doing needs be met at work, even though work is the natural center for doing. We must still leave time for nonwork, usually nonmoney generating activities like hobbies and special interests. No matter how rewarding, how can work match the joy of the amateur musician's first studio recording, the gourmet cook's latest mouth-watering creation, or the cross-country bicycle race? To sacrifice these activities upon the altar of work responsibilities eventually predicts an increase in a person's dissatisfaction with life and greater probability that they will become angry.

My goal in this book is to help readers get along better at work. This chapter's theme has been on getting along by preventing useless anger and harmful conflicts. However, some anger does need to be expressed and some conflicts do have to be addressed. That leads to the topic of the next chapter: reducing one's anger and conflict to manageable levels.

3

Anger and Conflict Reduction

Communication Breakdown and Loss of Control

A state of hatred has been declared within the nursing department at Happy Endings Nursing Home. Three long-time nurses won't talk anymore with the new head of the department, Nellie Moore. It all began when Ms. Moore changed the nurses' hours without consulting with them. But that single event is history now. It's just one of dozens of complaints the nurses have lodged against Ms. Moore. What else is history are any attempts to mend the situation. The other nurses quit trying to fix things weeks ago. They claim Ms. Moore never listens to them anyhow, so why should they bother? Meanwhile, Nellie Moore has dug in her heels. "I don't care what they think of me," she says, "I'm the head nurse and they better get used to it." The conflict has become an "Either she goes or we go" crisis situation, even though no one intended for it to go that far. Feelings are running so high that almost everyone has gotten caught up in the mess, even some of the residents. It seems that just about all the parties to this conflict have lost control of their emotions. Common sense has been forsaken. Each participant in this conflict is trapped, unable to figure out ways to de-escalate the problem.

The conflict at Happy Endings has taken on a life of its own. It's out of control now, like a forest fire being whipped up by sixty mile an hour winds. The most likely result is that some people will have to leave and lingering resentments will disrupt morale for months to come. This all too common pattern is the result of a failure to control the intensity level of a conflict.

Conflicts are usually productive as long as the parties in the conflict maintain effective contact with each other. This line of communication is easily threatened, however. Indeed, it can be severed completely, a disastrous situation that usually leads to intense and damaging battles.

This chapter has two parts. First, we'll examine the process of conflict escalation—the ways intensity builds up in conflict until productive resolution becomes impossible. The second part of the chapter is devoted to ways to reduce the intensity of conflict.

The Process of Conflict Escalation

Probably almost every worker could lose control of their emotions under certain circumstances. First one thing goes wrong. Then another and another. Frustration starts to build, which produces physical and emotional tension. The tension comes out as irritability that gradually becomes outright anger. Becoming more and more angry, the person makes poor choices, such as making accusations or calling names. That bothers others and only makes the situation worse. Finally the worker completely blows up, yelling and screaming or even physically attacking objects or people. It's important to understand how anger and conflict builds so that this unfortunate chain of events can be stopped.

This sequence may, and often does, begin with a legitimate concern. For example, the conflict at Happy Endings Nursing Home began when Ms. Moore, the new head nurse, decided to change people's hours without talking to them. However, the process of losing control can still occur regardless of whether or not the initial concern is real. It's not what you disagree about but *how* you disagree that is crucial. Conflicts escalate into disasters when they are poorly handled.

The process of loss of control has many components. The most important are these:

- At the emotional level, people become hotheaded. They become more and more angry as annoyance becomes anger that turns into rage. As intensity increases, the possibility for reasonable discussion decreases.

- At the cognitive level, people quit thinking clearly. They interpret each others' actions and words negatively, refusing to give the other person the benefit of the doubt. Paranoia creeps in as good judgment decreases.

- At the behavioral level, people become both more impulsive and more explosive. They do things without thinking that they would never do if they had better control.

- At the moral level, people become rigid, dividing the world and their workplace into good and bad. Frequently, they become bitter and hostile, developing a severe case of mean-spiritedness toward others.

Losing Control of Your Emotions

Take a look at the Anger Thermometer on the next page. Notice how anger (and every other emotion) can be divided into four levels of intensity: low, medium, high, and extremely high. Each level of intensity has words usually associated with it, too:

- Low level anger—annoyed, irritated, bothered

- Medium level anger—angry, mad, "pissed"

- High level anger—irate, fuming, furious

- Extremely high level anger—enraged, hateful, boiling

You Can Get Too Angry

As your anger heats up, so does your body. The fight or flight response kicks in, adrenaline rushes through your system, your voice gets higher and louder, you may begin to pace, your hands tend to curl into fists, your face may become distorted into a thin-lipped grimace. Your whole body becomes transformed as you prepare physically and emotionally to attack or to defend yourself. You literally feel mad. You are now ready to blow.

Anger Thermometer

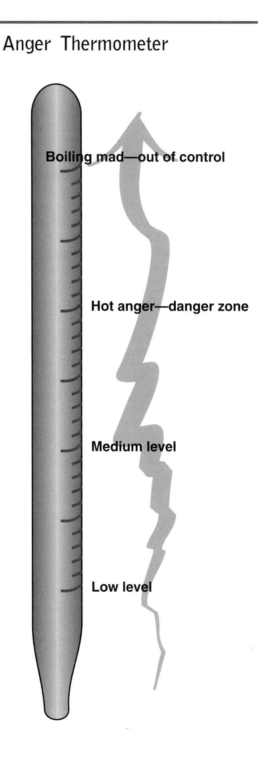

Boiling mad—out of control

Hot anger—danger zone

Medium level

Low level

In the 1970s and 1980s many writers encouraged periodic anger blowups as a way to stay healthy. The idea was to ventilate your anger so that it wouldn't make you sick. Unexpressed anger was thought inevitably to pile up inside people until they would either became ill or explode. Besides, it was believed that most people would feel better after they ventilated their anger.

That piece of advice, to fully and strongly express one's anger, is seldom given anymore. The reason is that newer research (see Tavris' *Anger: The Misunderstood Emotion*, 1989) clearly shows that "letting it all out" has many negative effects, including disapproval from others. But the worst effect of ventilation is that it teaches people to become more angry over time. The cost of ventilating one's anger too frequently is that the anger actually builds up rather than lessens. In other words, the more often you let yourself get really angry, the better you train yourself to become angry.

Too frequent ventilation of anger leads to becoming more angry, not less. The final result may be someone who develops a habit of anger. This person tends to react to almost everything with anger, both at work and home. Not only does he or she get angry about everything from a knock on the office door to a rumor of layoffs but they become *intensely* angry. Irate, furious, fuming, the chronically angry person continually activates the body's fight or flight response. That makes them a prime candidate for a heart attack or stroke, and indeed, chronically angry and hostile individuals tend to suffer far more heart problems and consequently die considerably younger than less angry people (Williams and Williams, 1994).

Legitimate anger is a signal that something is wrong. It does need to be noticed and addressed. But it's important to keep the level of intensity down. Becoming too angry is dangerous to your health.

How Too Much Anger Affects Your Thinking

There is another big problem with intense anger: Communications usually break down when people become too intensely upset. Dialogues become monologues. People cannot simultaneously shout at each other and solve their conflicts. Imagine what would happen if Ms. Moore of the Happy Endings Nursing Home and her staff tried to settle their differences while screaming at the top of their lungs. They would only frustrate each other and become even more convinced that there were no solutions.

Communications break down because intense anger affects a person's ability to think clearly in several ways. First, it's difficult to process complex information when you're angry. That means angry people will oversimplify the situation. For example, the angrier Nellie Moore gets the more she says things like this at the nursing home: "It's a simple black and white issue. I have the right to change my staff's hours, and that's that." When she's less angry, though, Nellie can think of more issues: "Yes, I have that right. But I remember when I was on line and how important it was for me to control my hours. Maybe we can work something out."

Another "thought problem" that crops up when people get angry is the overly negative interpretation of others' words and deeds. In particular, angry people often interpret neutral comments as hostile ones. Let's say that Bob Martin, the assistant nurse, asks Ms. Moore if she's completed next month's schedule. That's a neutral question, but the more angry Nellie is, the more likely she'll think she's being attacked or accused of doing something bad. Then she'll get defensive and perhaps say something like, "Mind your own business, Bob. I'll get that schedule out when I'm good and ready to," only convincing the others even more that she's impossible to work with.

Cognitive rigidity is a third likely result of getting too angry. "Do it my way or else"; "I'm right and they're wrong"; "First you make out the Z file. Then the Q file. Then the L file. That's the way we do things around here, so don't ask any more questions." Rigid, angry thinking makes it much harder to reach compromises or negotiated agreements.

Two more thought problems really kick in when anger becomes too intense. First, people start to obsess. They can't quit thinking about their conflicts. Nellie Moore, for instance, just can't stop thinking about her work battles even after she goes home. She tries to play with her children and talk with her husband, Tim. But then she hears herself beginning to complain about the other nurses, right in the middle of supper or a card game. Even her husband Tim's bored "here she goes again" sigh fails to deter her. It's as if those other nurses have taken up permanent residence inside her brain.

Paranoia is the second indicator that anger and conflict have gotten out of control. That's when you begin thinking that others are out to get you, that they must spend hours every day plotting how to make your work time miserable. Sometimes it seems that just a few people are collaborating against you ("You know, my manager has been trying to get rid of me for years. Now he's got the foremen on his side, and all they do is look for my mistakes"). Worse, you might believe that they're all against you. Either way, a predictable result is that the paranoid worker becomes more suspicious, defensive, isolated, and hostile. Ms. Moore, feeling attacked on all sides, might retreat to her office, venturing out infrequently and hardly ever socializing with her staff.

Anger Affects Your Behavior

Impulsive and *excessive*. These are the key words that describe the likely actions of someone who has become too intensely angry at work.

Impulsive. "That's it. I quit!" So shouts Bob Martin, the assistant head nurse at Happy Endings, after another run-in with Nellie Moore. He sure means what he says now, but he'll regret it later.

Excessive. "I marched into Moore's office and told her off. I said she could kiss my ass if she thinks I'm gonna work one more weekend a month. I'm not gonna let her push me around any longer. I was so mad, I tore up the work schedule right in her face." Thus remarks Ann Campbell, the about-to-be-suspended night nurse at Happy Endings. Later, she too will regret the way she chose to protest.

Probably neither of these frustrated workers would normally act so thoughtlessly. Now, both have further damaged their relationships with their boss and perhaps jeopardized their professional careers. That's why it's important to be careful when you're upset and to be extra cautious when you're really angry. Beware of the twin dangers of impulsive and excessive action during conflict. Both types of behavior only serve to intensify conflicts while lessening the likelihood for positive problem resolution.

Moral Rigidity and Warfare

Nellie Moore's had it with her staff. As far as she's concerned, they are "The Evil Enemy." They're lazy, stupid, vicious, arrogant, incompetent, awful, and bad. She'd fire every last one if she could, replacing them with people who were willing to work harder and better.

It's just as bad on the other side. Bob Martin, Ann Campbell, and most of the other nurses wouldn't say anything decent about Nellie Moore if you paid them to. They decided a long time ago that

Moore is pushy, a control freak, a management toady, nasty, ugly, and morally corrupt. The rest of management is just as bad, they tell each other, because they refuse to fire Moore.

War time. A fight to the death. Good vs. evil. Note that both sides are certain they are morally right. Each is certain that any reasonable person would take their side in the conflict. "We're good and they're bad. It's that simple." But life is seldom that clear. Just like everyone else, Nellie Moore has both positive and negative characteristics. So do Bob Martin, Ann Campbell, and all the rest. The trouble is that these workers have become polarized. They no longer can recognize the good traits of their opponents, much less the validity of any suggestions made by the others. Both sides have become morally rigid, locked into a narrow and destructive perception of the universe.

It's almost certain that negotiations at Happy Endings will fall apart now. Who would give in, even over a minor issue, to "one of them"? Who would be able to back off and try to look at things from a more objective position? Moral rigidity leads to stalled talks, standoffs, and stalemates.

People suffer when work becomes a war zone. Bitterness and meanness of spirit are the final results of overly intense anger and conflict, especially when the conflicts are both strong and long lasting. Workers become embittered both because of the nasty things people say and do to them and also because of the nasty things they say and do to others. Excessive conflict brings out the worst in people.

Anger and conflict have their place at work. The goal, though, is to guard against that anger becoming either too intense or prolonged. The rest of this chapter offers ways to reduce the intensity of anger and conflict so that it stays manageable.

Living by the Principles of Moderation

Joe Longstreet decided to bake cookies for the company Christmas party. Unfortunately, Joe grew up never having to cook. So, when the recipe said to turn the oven to three hundred degrees for twenty minutes he reasoned that they ought to bake just fine if he set the heat at six hundred degrees for ten minutes. They burned so badly that it took him weeks to get the burnt smell out of his kitchen.

Did Joe learn his lesson? Not quite. The next time he decided to be extra careful not to burn the cookies. Instead of three hundred degrees for twenty minutes, he set the oven for one-hundred-and-fifty degrees for forty minutes. The result was a soggy mass of under-cooked dough.

Joe's debacle isn't only about cookies, though. His problem is that he ignored the principle of moderation, namely that *most things work best when approached with a moderate amount of energy.* Joe applied too much heat too quickly, then too little heat too slowly. It's exactly those two tendencies—too much heat too quickly and too little heat too slowly—that must be changed in order to handle anger at work well.

"Moderation: avoiding extremes of behavior or expression."

"To moderate: to lessen intensity or extremeness."

These definitions of the concept of moderation (from Webster's Seventh New Collegiate Dictionary, 1965) describe the main principle we can use to help reduce the intensity of both our own and others' anger and conflict in the workplace.

First, we must individually learn to live by the principle of moderation. This means recognizing that a certain amount of anger and conflict is normal. Once in a while, almost everyone is going to get upset over something. You probably aren't an exception. A little anger once in a while is not a problem, as long as that anger is well-handled. However, a lot of anger and conflict, even if that anger only lasts a few minutes, is a problem. It's even worse if you become very angry over a long time period. The idea behind the principle of moderation is to keep anger from becoming excessive—or to get it back to a manageable level if it's already become intensified.

Second, perhaps you can learn not only to control your own anger but also to help others with theirs. That's when you become a moderator, the person others can come to when they need to get a realistic view of their situation or when they need someone to help them calm down a bit.

There are four main ways to handle workplace anger and conflict through the principle of moderation:

- Keep your body calm.

- Keep your mind open.

- Keep your actions reasonable.

- Look for the good in others.

Keep Your Body Calm

Nellie Moore's husband, Tim, was giving Nellie a good-bye hug one morning when he mentioned that her back muscles were tight. That's when Nellie realized how her body had become like a suit of armor she put on every morning before she went to work and only sometimes was able to remove at night. She then started noticing more bodily signs of chronic anger and anxiety: taking shallow breaths, a heavy feeling in her chest, frequent headaches, walking with a guarded "I've always got to watch for danger" step. And all that was before she even got to work. Once there she noticed another alarming bodily response: Where before people had always commented on her expansive gestures, the way she took up all the space around her with her flowing arms, now she was making much smaller gestures, as if her arms would get chopped off if they strayed too far from her trunk.

Then Nellie took a good look at her face in the mirror. When had she developed that frown? Those pinched-together eyes? That blank stare? Nor did she like the sound of her voice when she spoke with the other nurses: a little too loud, too high, unnatural. Furthermore, she paced rapidly in their presence, unable to slow herself down long enough really to listen to their words.

Notice that Nellie, like many workers, is trying to deal with two emotions at the same time. She's both angry and afraid. This combination of fear and anger is quite common. Instead of fight or flight the body wants to do both at the same time. This fight *and* flight reaction may produce erratic and unpredictable behaviors. Nellie may be overly aggressive one day, overly timid the next.

What, then, can you do if you are faced with a similar situation, one in which a certain amount of conflict cannot be avoided and which triggers this fight and flight reaction? The answer is that you need to relax your face and body. *Relaxation, fortunately, reduces both the urge to fight and to flee.*

Before you can relax effectively, though, you need to do a little research. There's one crucial question to answer: Where in your body do you feel your anger and anxiety? In your eyes? Jaw? Chest? Stomach? Hands? Legs? Back? Lungs? Heart? Your whole body? And how does your body show your anger and anxiety to others? With your voice? Your gestures? Your pace? Your glare? The places you locate are exactly those that you'll need to relax if you want to lessen your anger and anxiety.

Relaxation is a skill you can teach yourself. It's useful both before and during a conflict. Before a conflict, relaxing helps give you a sense of personal control and empowerment. During a conflict, relaxing helps you stay focused upon problems without becoming distracted by your own body. The only catch with relaxation is that you have to practice it to perfect it. You can't just say to yourself "now just relax." You also have to know how to relax the unique instrument that is your body. You might choose to read a book such as *The Relaxation and Stress Reduction Workbook* (Davis, Robbins, and McKay 1995) or sign up for some relaxation training to increase your relaxation knowledge and skill.

Here, though, are some immediate guidelines to relax your body in the face of a conflictual situation:

- Start by giving yourself this important message: "I can handle conflict at work and stay relaxed." Giving yourself this message is especially crucial if you've come to associate work conflict with getting nervous, angry, or agitated. Basically, you've got to break the conflict/anxious-angry connection both in your mind and body.

- Breathe slowly, gently, deeply. Most people cut their breath off when they're upset. Rapid, shallow breathing only increases agitation and decreases your ability to handle conflict. If you can't take in air, how can you take in the energy you need in difficult situations? No matter how heavy the action, it's always possible to slow your body down by taking several deep breaths while reminding yourself to relax.

- First, relax the areas of your body that respond most quickly. Perhaps you've discovered that when you're bothered you tend to clamp your jaw, tighten your back muscles, and make fists. Of the three, the one that you can change quickest is your jaw. So go there first, letting your jaw muscles loosen a bit to the point where your teeth aren't clamping against each other. Then go on to the other areas, if you have time.

- Pay special attention to your face. Facial muscles are particularly important because they send signals both to others and back to your own brain. Since your face tells everybody (including yourself) what's going on, it's important not to convey messages like "Right now I feel like strangling you."

Besides, people are relatively more used to manipulating facial muscles than many others. That makes it easier to relax your face than most other areas of your body.

- Develop your own special thirty-second work relaxation routine. Work gets much less stressful when you have regular stretching, breathing, and/or mind-relaxing rituals that you use regularly either before or at the first signs of developing tension. If you let yourself take three or four half-minute relaxation breaks each day, you will almost certainly notice that you're generally less anxious and angry.

Keep Your Mind Open

Ann Campbell, the night nurse at Happy Endings, is a little upset with herself. "I've done it again," she says. "I got hooked into the battle between Nellie and Bob. Now I'm acting just as dumb as them." Ann doesn't like how she feels. She needs to relax. Most of all, though, Ann is unhappy with how she's been thinking about the situation. Some of her thoughts (like the notion that management hired Mrs. Moore so she could find a way to get rid of Ann) really don't make sense to her when she's calm. She realizes she needs to review not only what she says to herself but also the irrational manner of her thinking at the nursing home.

Earlier in this chapter I mentioned five cognitive problems that greatly hinder a person's ability to think effectively when a conflict develops. These are oversimplification, negative interpretation, rigidity, obsession, and paranoia. These problems tend to develop during conflict even among people who normally think quite clearly. The longer the conflict lasts and the more intense it becomes, the more likely it is that people will begin thinking in ways that only ensure the conflict will get worse. The general principle is that rational, effective, problem-solving thinking gradually becomes replaced by irrational, ineffective, problem-increasing thinking during intense or prolonged periods of stress, anxiety, and conflict. This tendency can be countered, however, but only if the participants in the conflict are committed to keep thinking clearly. Here are some ways to help you do just that.

Combating Oversimplification

Get all the facts. Don't jump to conclusions. Make no assumptions based on the past. Don't rush toward "obvious" solutions. Seek "both/and" rather than "either/or" answers.

Ann Campbell had been thinking that Mrs. Moore wanted to change their schedules just because Nellie likes power and control. But Ann knows people are complex and complicated. Yes, maybe Nellie likes power and control, but there are certainly many other possible reasons for her actions. The point is that Ann's never even tried to find out what those reasons are. She's assumed she knew the facts. She didn't think to ask Nellie why she wanted to change their schedules. If she had, she'd have discovered that Nellie thought she could help the staff function more efficiently and that Nellie believed proper patient care was endangered by the current way the nurses were scheduled.

People are complicated. Situations that produce conflict at work are usually complex. Additionally, solutions to conflicts often involve negotiation and compromise. It's seldom that one side or the other just plain wins. Rather, conflict participants need to be able to seek solutions that are good enough and fair enough for everyone to live by.

Some of the questions you need to ask yourself during a conflict, especially if it seems to be getting out of control, are these: Am I keeping an open mind? Am I oversimplifying? Am I making assumptions without checking the facts? Am I willing to look at the situation differently than I have been? Am I leaving anything out?

Stopping Negative Interpretation

Let neutral statements stay neutral; give people the benefit of the doubt; ask neutral parties for a more objective view.

Imagine this scene at home:

Mom: Please pass the salt.

Dad: Well, what do you mean by that? Are you saying I'm impolite because I put salt on my food first?

Son:	Yeah, Dad, she always does that. She's putting you down.
Mom:	Hey, all I said was pass the salt. Why are you making such a big deal out of it?

Ridiculous? Actually scenes like this happen all the time when people are angry and mistrusting of each other. They happen at work, too:

Bill:	Man, I had to work two extra hours last night to finish that Jones file.
Al:	Sure, just at bonus time. I bet you did that just to show us up.
Marti:	Yeah, that pisses me off. Besides, I need some overtime. Why'd the boss ask you and not me?
Bill:	All I did was work a couple of extra hours. Why are you getting so upset?

Anything someone says or does can be appraised by others as being good, neutral, or bad. In general the greater the anger and conflict going on the more likely that people will interpret each other's behavior negatively. Since probably over 90 percent of our day-to-day remarks and actions are neutral, neither good nor bad, that means that many of those neutral remarks and behaviors will be mistakenly appraised as bad. (See the diagram on the next page.)

This negative appraisal pattern is unintentional. It's a gradual process that creeps in during periods of stress and conflict. The way to resist this shift is to remind yourself that most comments are simple exchanges of information, neither good nor bad. It's important not to look for hidden or negative meanings in these exchanges. Let neutral stay neutral, and you'll avoid a lot of unnecessary grief.

It also helps to give people the benefit of the doubt. That means edging yourself a little toward the positive interpretation side of the appraisal scale. Okay, maybe you could interpret your coworker's remark as a put-down. But, what good will that do? Give them the benefit of the doubt. Assume someone's acting in good faith until proven otherwise. Giving others the benefit of the doubt is especially important when there is conflict in the workplace. It's a good way of refusing to get sucked into an atmosphere of criticism and hostility.

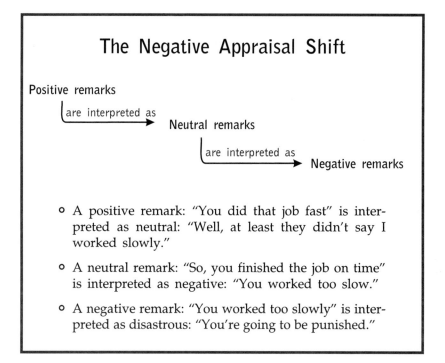

The Negative Appraisal Shift

Positive remarks

are interpreted as

→ Neutral remarks

are interpreted as

→ Negative remarks

o A positive remark: "You did that job fast" is interpreted as neutral: "Well, at least they didn't say I worked slowly."

o A neutral remark: "So, you finished the job on time" is interpreted as negative: "You worked too slow."

o A negative remark: "You worked too slowly" is interpreted as disastrous: "You're going to be punished."

A third tactic to lessen negative thinking is to ask neutral parties for their interpretations of difficult situations. That doesn't mean trying to convince them that your opponent is a jerk, though. The idea isn't to gather allies but to make sure that you're not creating false problems for yourself. Neutral parties might include fellow workers who aren't involved in a particular dispute, people you know are friendly both toward you and to the other person, or perhaps an Employee Assistance Program professional whose job is to help people sort things out.

Relaxing Your Thinking

Identify and challenge your rigid thinking habits that increase conflict. Reduce negative labeling by looking for exceptions. Avoid the words "always" and "never." Put yourself in the other person's shoes (be more empathic).

Bob Martin, the assistant head nurse at Happy Endings, has always had a problem with rigid thinking patterns. Specifically, he suffers from "My way or the highway" thinking. It seems so obvious to him that there's only one right way to do anything, that he knows the right way, and that anybody who opposes him is wrong. This is one reason the scheduling conflict overheated; Bob refused to back down from his position that the old way (which he helped design) was the best way.

It's easy to get locked into rigid, counterproductive, conflict increasing ways of thinking at work. But these thinking patterns can be changed. The trick is first to identify these habits and then to challenge them. Bob Martin, for instance, could help himself by accepting that other people often have good ideas and then by actually listening to their suggestions.

Mental rigidity acts like a lock on the door of your mind. Ask yourself these questions to help unlock it:

- Are there any topics or issues at work where I've simply made up my mind and that's that?

- Are there any people at work whose thoughts and suggestions I automatically ignore or belittle?

- Have I gotten stuck in ways of thinking that are increasing problems and tension at work?

If your answer to any of these questions is "yes," you should ask yourself if you're willing to make the effort to re-open your mind. If so, you'll need to consider new input about previously closed topics and really listen to people you've been ignoring.

Negative labeling, such as deciding someone is stupid, incompetent, worthless, or bad, is a sign of mental rigidity. It helps to look for exceptions when you're trying to break this pattern. For example, you might believe that one of your coworkers is lazy. But then you notice him volunteering to carry some heavy packages into the storage room. Guess he's not as lazy as you thought. The less you negatively label, the better you will be at dealing with conflictual or stressful situations as they arise.

Beware of the words "always" and "never," as in "She always comes in late" or "He never does his share." These two words are usually exaggerations that increase anger and conflict whenever you think or say them. They are usually signs of extreme negative labeling.

Finally, practice empathy. Empathy is the art of stepping away from your viewpoint in order to see a situation through another's eyes and mind. Unfortunately, empathy becomes harder to do in direct proportion to the intensity and duration of conflict. The angrier you are, in other words, the less you can see things from the other's point of view. That's why you have to make a conscious effort to be more empathic during conflict, just when you least want to. You must remember to ask yourself these questions when you are in a conflict situation:

- If I were him/her, what would be important right now?

- If I were him/her, what would I want and need?

- If I were him/her, what would I be feeling?

- If I were him/her, what would bother me the most about what others are saying and doing?

- If I were him/her, what would help me feel appreciated?

Minimizing Obsessional and Paranoid Thoughts

Don't let dialogues turn into double monologues. Use thought stopping and thought substitution to diminish obsession. Choose to step away from your own and group paranoia.

The goal of this chapter is to lower the heat in the face of real conflict so that resolutions are possible. One sure sign that the heat is rising, though, is when people become so involved in their own thoughts that they no longer can hear what others are saying. Dialogues then become double monologues: each person talks *at* the other person rather than *with* them. This is when the number of interruptions increase—people start thinking about what they're going to say long before the other person is done, and conversations begin sounding like broken records as people continually repeat their messages. The messages aren't modified in light of the other's response because nobody is listening to that response. Double monologues increase everybody's frustration. Each party notices, correctly, that the other person really isn't listening to them. Of course, it's harder for each individual to notice that they're doing the same thing.

Two habits of thinking greatly increase the likelihood for double monologues. These are obsession and paranoia. Obsession means to think repeatedly about something that is usually bad, dangerous, or upsetting. Paranoia means to be irrationally or excessively suspicious or distrusting.

Nellie Moore has become obsessive about the scheduling crisis at Happy Endings. "All I can think about is that stupid schedule," she complains to her husband. Nellie can't get it out of her mind. At home, she can't read a book, balance her checking account, or even make love without getting distracted by thoughts of scheduling. At work, it seems that every conversation, no matter how remote, soon leads to scheduling. Furthermore, the more she thinks about scheduling, the more anxious she gets.

Ann Campbell, the night nurse, has always been a little suspicious and distrusting. But by now, after a few months of work conflict, Ann's become considerably more paranoid. She's only certain these days about one thing: Don't trust anybody at work. Who knows when one of the other nurses will spread gossip? Who can really say who is on whose side anymore? When will management start laying people off? Is Nellie Moore looking for reasons to fire her?

The first step in ending double monologues is to make a personal commitment to hear others. That means quieting your desire to speak long enough to listen. It means responding to their concerns before going on to yours. It also means listening for new information that might help solve a problem or end a conflict. Finally, making a commitment to listen might mean being patient with others who are stuck in their own repetitions and obsessions. Remember that you are only in charge of your own thoughts and words. You can't make another person quit double monologuing. However, you can stop doing that yourself, and it's probable that your choice will eventually influence others in your organization.

Thought stopping and thought substitution are particularly useful ways to break obsessive thinking patterns. Thought stopping means gently but firmly telling yourself to quit thinking about something you've been obsessing about whenever it interferes with the rest of your life. Thought substitution allows you to decide what else you want to think about. Nellie Moore would practice these techniques by saying to herself something like this: "Now, Nellie, cut it out. I don't have to think about scheduling right now. I'll think about what to tell Mrs. Jackson's children when they come to visit instead." Sure, those scheduling thoughts will soon try to creep back into her mind. But Nellie will gain freedom every time she can block them and substitute new thoughts. She'll become less anxious, too. Then, when she does have to deal with scheduling, she may very well come up with some new ways to deal with the situation.

Paranoia may be even harder to root out than obsession. That's because people can always find things to be suspicious and distrusting about when they go looking for them. Also, one person's doubts often feed another's, so that entire work groups can become irrationally distrusting. But, when the goal is to keep conflict from getting out of hand, it's vitally important to step away from that paranoia. Imagine that the paranoia is a snarling, growling dog ready to attack anybody in sight. The idea is to step around the dog so you're not bitten by paranoia.

To minimize paranoia you must tell yourself these statements:

- "No, everybody isn't out to get me."

- "Getting paranoid will only make the situation worse."

- "If I only look for things to get defensive about, then I will only find things to get defensive about."

- "I can choose to trust people."

- "I won't join in when others are getting paranoid. Instead, I'll make my own decisions about who I can trust."

Keep Your Actions Reasonable

Loss of control usually consists of two kinds of behavior: excessive and impulsive. Excessive behaviors are too strong; impulsive actions are too quick. Instead of "too little, too late" the action here is "too much, too soon." Alone, workers with either of these tendencies might have problems. Together, workers with both excessive and impulsive tendencies often say or do things they deeply regret.

Loss of control doesn't just happen by accident. Almost always there is a buildup period—a time when your anger gradually escalates. Even though the immediate incident may appear to be spontaneous—such as when one worker suddenly "snaps" and threatens to strangle another—normally it turns out there is a long history of unresolved conflicts, hurt feelings, and grievances.

Loss of control is often a shared pattern. It's not just that Bob Martin, the assistant head nurse, is edgy and ready to blow. So is his boss, Nellie Moore, and the night nurse, Ann Campbell. They are involved in a mutual escalation process. Each time one of them "goes off," that person encourages the others to do the same. They are training each other to become more and more unreasonable, explosive, and aggressive. Furthermore, after a while they learn exactly how to trigger each other's explosions. It's bad enough that over time each of them has become a firecracker. In addition, they have also become each other's matchboxes.

It's possible to guard against getting swept up in this mutual hostility pattern. Indeed, that's the whole idea of this chapter. In order to do so you will need to do three things:

- Observe your own and your group's conflict escalation processes.

- Learn how to slow down your behaviors to avoid impulsive action errors.

- Learn how to tone down your behaviors to avoid excessive action errors.

Observe Conflict Escalation Processes

Conflict escalations consist of linked sets of gradually intensifying thoughts, bodily sensations, and actions. Nellie Moore, for example, may have the following sets:

- *Lower-stage thought:* I'm annoyed that Bob's trying to change the schedule again.

- *Lower-stage bodily sensation:* My neck muscles feel tight.

- *Lower-stage action:* I'll ask Bob to leave the schedule as it is.

- *Middle-stage thought:* I'm angry because he's always meddling in my business.

- *Middle-stage bodily sensation:* Now my stomach's starting to knot up.

- *Middle-stage action:* I'm gonna put out a memo telling everybody that I won't change the schedule no matter who complains about it. Bob will get the message to butt out.

- *Higher-stage thought:* I won't put up with his insubordination one minute more!

- *Higher-stage bodily sensation:* My heart's racing, my head's pounding, my gut's aching.

- *Higher-stage action:* I'm marching right down to his office to give him a piece of my mind.

- *Out-of-control thought:* I hate him! He's history. It's me or him.

- *Out-of-control bodily sensations:* I feel like I'm gonna explode. I can't stop shaking.

- *Out-of-control action:* Why am I yelling like this? What's happening to me?

Most people's escalation paths are predictable, especially in a limited setting like work, where frustrations occur in regular patterns. People usually go through the same or very similar sets of thoughts, sensations, and actions each time they explode. But that very predictability makes it easier to keep from losing control. All you have to do is recognize when you're beginning to lose control before you actually do so and then break the routine by changing your thoughts, sensations, or actions. Since I've already discussed ways to change your bodily sensations and thoughts earlier in this chapter, the rest of this section will focus upon how to alter your actions.

You can learn to recognize your personal conflict escalation path. One way is by taking the time to write out your own groups of linked sets of thoughts, sensations and actions. Your paper would look like this:

First I think _____

and my body feels _____

and I do _____

Then next I think _____

and my body feels _____

and I do _____

Until finally I think _____

and my body feels _____

and I do _____

You may want to work backwards because sometimes it's hard to remember what the earlier parts of the sequence are like. In that case begin with your explosion:

The last thing I thought was _____

The last thing my body felt was _____

The last thing I did was _____

Right before that I thought _____

and my body felt _____

and I did _____

You also might need a little help. Sometimes others can remind you of things you said and did that you've forgotten in the heat of your explosion.

It's equally important to chart any mutual escalations in which you participate. Keep the focus upon actions here, though, since it's dangerous to try to guess what others are thinking and feeling. Your paper will look like this:

First I said/did _____

Then he/she said/did _____

Then I said/did _____

And he/she said/did _____

Until finally I said/did _____

And he/she said/did _____

Slow Down to Avoid Impulsive Errors

Bob Martin's done it again. This time he shouted at Phyllis Watson, the owner of the nursing home, that he would quit unless she immediately fired Nellie Moore. Now he's back in his office kicking himself for being a fool. The sign over his desk reading "Think before you speak" is small consolation. Why hadn't he remembered that saying a few minutes ago? Bob's always had a short fuse. Unfortunately, the battling at Happy Endings seems to have made it even shorter.

If only conflict brought out the best in people. Then impatient individuals would become more patient instead of less. Instead, conflict tends to bring out or increase our weak points. In Bob's situation his impatience at work triggers impulsive, thoughtless actions that get him into trouble. But people can learn ways to be less impatient and impulsive. Here are a few guidelines to do just that:

1. Take responsibility for your words and actions *before* you say and do them. Don't be like Bob Martin, realizing too late that he's blown it again. The best way to avoid all the guilt and apologies that come with impulsive acts is to avoid them in the first place.

2. Buy time. Practice waiting five minutes before you act. Ask yourself two times if you really need to say something before you speak. If it's something that will get you into trouble or increase conflict, ask yourself at least three times before you speak. Another question to ask yourself is whether what you say or do will increase or decrease the current level of tension and conflict. Still another question is whether what you're thinking of saying or doing will increase or decrease your respect for yourself.

3. Take a "time-out" if you're losing control. This means leaving the scene for a while so you can calm down. Maybe all you'll need to do is to step away a few feet for a minute or two. Perhaps it means retreating to your office, cubicle, or truck for a break. It's important that you do something that helps cool you off during your break, though. A time-out is pretty useless if you only use it to work yourself into a "They can't do that to me!" rage. Also, don't go back into the stressful situation until you know you can keep in control even if others are still angry, bossy, or annoying. When you do return, try to focus your attention on problem solving so your anger doesn't get hooked again.

Avoid Excessive Action Errors

Bob Martin made two mistakes when he threatened to quit his job at Happy Endings. First, he spoke too hastily, as noted above. Secondly, he spoke too strongly. Bob only succeeded in painting himself into a corner by threatening to quit over a relatively small issue.

It's all too easy to say or do something in the midst of conflict that seems perfectly appropriate, only later to realize that you overreacted. But by then damage may have been done to your reputation and relationships. Fortunately, there are some things you can do to minimize the risk of taking excessively strong action.

Keep things in perspective. Making a bad situation worse leads to excessive action. That angry memo to the boss, the screaming bout with a coworker, or even the wrestling match with a crew member doesn't have to happen. It will, though, unless you remember to keep things in perspective.

Most often people react overaggressively when they feel personally or professionally attacked. But remember, it's easy to overestimate the severity of an attack. The key question to ask is this: On a scale of one to ten, how badly does another's behavior affect you? Base your answer on the following ratings:

10	Life threatening. My health and safety is at risk.
9–8	Critical. The other's behavior makes it virtually impossible for me to do my job.
7–6	Distressing. The other's behavior makes it very difficult to function. Much of my energy goes into reacting to his/her actions.
5–4	Troublesome. The other's behavior significantly affects my ability to do my job.
3–2	Annoying. The other's behavior makes doing my job a little more difficult, time consuming, or unpleasant.
1	Trivial. The other's behavior doesn't affect me personally or professionally.

Most attacks turn out to be mere annoyances: people making catty remarks, delaying your work a few minutes by being late, thoughtlessly changing a setting on a machine without consulting you, or being critical without knowing what they're talking about.

Big deal. Life is full of less than totally pleasant characters. The point is that these behaviors only affect you if you let them get to you or if you mistakenly believe they are more serious than they really are.

However, some attacks are indeed more serious. The scale rises as someone's behavior increasingly keeps you from working well and comfortably. Thus, someone's simply *annoying* habit of making sexual innuendoes in the lunchroom may become *troublesome* when they start making those hints directly to you, as that could affect your peace of mind and make your work environment feel less safe. That troublesome behavior may become *distressing* to you if the person refuses to quit when asked and *critical* when they become hostile and abrasive about it. Finally, you might very well feel the situation is *life threatening* if they were strongly to hint that they intend to hurt or assault you.

Here's another set. It might be *annoying* to have your coworker show up at your shared work site with a mild hangover, since it would slow down work a little. However, that coworker's behavior becomes *troublesome* if he's also angry and belligerent toward you, *distressing* if he sneaks off to the bathroom for more liquor so you have to do part of his job as well as yours, *critical* if his alcohol-affected work makes it impossible for you to complete the project, and *life threatening* if the two of you are trying to handle dangerous machinery while he's intoxicated.

Base your actions on the actual degree of severity of the problem. In other words, most of the time you would choose not to react at all to a trivial conflict while responding mildly to an annoying problem and gradually more strongly to troublesome, distressing, critical, and life-threatening ones. For example, you might shrug off your coworker's mild hangover, avoid him if he becomes surly, warn him to quit playing games if he keeps sneaking off, tell him to go home if he keeps drinking, and refuse to work with him on dangerous machinery even though that means getting him into trouble.

The idea is to keep your response moderate and proportionate to the problem. Of course, that isn't easy because conflicts can be so emotional. But when you can do it, you'll save yourself from having overreacted. That's one way to ensure that your reaction doesn't become viewed by others as their real problem instead of your initial concern.

Help others control their potentially impulsive and excessive actions. One day Ann Campbell and Bob Martin were joking that they should form a "PFIM" club. PFIM stands for "place foot in mouth," something they both do well. Then they got serious. They decided never to say or do anything until each could check things out with the other. Since they work different shifts, that simple decision bought time and helped prevent overreacting.

Everybody gets overly excited on occasion. That's when it's necessary to find someone you trust to talk things over. It's important, when someone from work seeks you out, that you assist them in slowing down to avoid impulsive errors and toning down to avoid overreacting. You can do so by helping them correctly decide how severe the problem is on the ten-point scale and then helping them plan an appropriate response. But, you'll need to keep a cool head in this process. Your least useful reaction would be to get swept up in the situation yourself. Remember that someone else's emergency doesn't have to become yours. You're under no obligation to hop a ride in the automobile of their life just when they're speeding out of control. Instead, you could remind them how to put on the brakes to avoid an unnecessary collision.

Look for the Good in Others

Moral rigidity, the tendency to see one side as all good and the other as all bad, is a common problem during workplace conflict. At Happy Endings, for instance, Nellie Moore eventually decided that her subordinates were all lazy and incompetent, while they in turn viewed her as controlling and corrupt.

Moral rigidity is a great contributor to the development of a "state of hate" within an organization. It's easy to despise people when you believe that they're evil and awful. It justifies treating them with contempt by ignoring them, belittling them, and verbally abusing them. Since one person's hate may trigger another's, entire organizations may eventually become trapped in hate. The whole workplace becomes mean-spirited. It's "us" vs. "them," now and forever. Moral rigidity, then, makes conflicts both last longer and become more intense.

There are three ways you can keep from becoming morally rigid at work. First, you need to remember to separate people from problems. The goal is to learn how to attack the problem and not the person. Second, you need to remember to look for the goodness in others, especially those with whom you disagree. Third, you have to learn how to let go of old resentments.

Separate People from Problems

I mentioned in chapter 3 that harmful conflicts are personality oriented. Workers in these situations tend to lose track of their real concerns. Instead, they begin attacking the other's character, style, and personality. People begin awfulizing and devilizing: they see others as totally terrible and bad. These personality attacks make it almost impossible to resolve issues. Work effectiveness generally plummets when people spend their time thinking and talking about how terrible their coworkers are.

There are several questions you can ask yourself to help you separate problems from persons:

1. Regardless of their personality, what is the nugget of truth I need to address in what the other person is saying or doing?

2. If this were my favorite coworker talking to me about this issue, what would I be able to hear better?

3. Am I tempted to disagree with this person mostly because of who they are rather than what they're saying?

4. Have I made someone into an enemy? If so, how is that affecting me, them, and the organization?

5. Am I remembering to separate the person from the problem?

6. What do I need to do to quit devilizing others?

7. How would I feel better about myself if I could quit devilizing?

Look for the Good in Others

Nellie Moore has decided to do something to lessen the fighting at Happy Endings. Wisely, she starts with herself. Realizing she's been paying attention only to what's wrong with her staff, Nellie makes a conscious effort to look for the good. That's when she really notices how much Bob Martin cares for the residents and that Ann Campbell is both thoughtful and considerate of her assistants.

People who awfulize and devilize look for the bad in others. That certainly increases conflict. However, it's not enough simply to quit awfulizing and devilizing to keep anger and conflict under control. You also have to remember to look for the good in others. It's usually fairly easy to find goodness once you start looking for it. After all, most people do far more good than harm in this world.

One problem, though, is letting go of the desire to look for the bad in others. There's a certain part of many people, the part that compares the self against others, which delights in finding fault. It's as if seeing how bad someone else is makes you better than them. The reasoning is something like this: "I need to feel good about myself. But if I'm good somebody has to be bad. I better look for badness in others because if they're not bad then I must be." This comparison process regularly gets worse when people disagree. Furthermore, the comparisons often become moralistic. Now the goal becomes proving that others are morally bad, evil, corrupt, dangerous. It's just so tempting to add the moral judgment ". . . and they're bad" to the factual statement "I disagree with them . . ."

The antidote for this kind of reasoning is to recognize that there really is enough goodness to go around. For instance, Nellie Moore doesn't have to be bad in order for Bob Martin to be good. Nor does Ann Campbell's goodness have to be a threat to Nellie. Instead, they could each choose to celebrate working with capable and caring colleagues.

The best time to cut off a moral judgment is before you make it, of course. But if that's not possible, if you find that you've already placed someone in your moral doghouse, then here is what you can do to change things around. First, remind yourself that there is much good in others. Second, tell yourself that the person or people you have judged so negatively are no exceptions to that idea. They, too, are good. Third, tell yourself on a regular basis that just because people disagree with you doesn't make them bad. Fourth, make yourself notice the good things they do instead of the bad. You'll need to do this for more than a couple minutes, by the way, since you've probably trained yourself to look for the bad for a long time. The result of this effort should be that you'll get along better with others because you no longer see them as morally bad.

Let Go of Old Resentments

It's taken weeks, but the fighting at Happy Endings is finally ending. People are treating each other more respectfully. They're even noticing the good things they each do. But there's still a current of anger and conflict, a dangerous undertow ready to pull the staff deep into the ocean of rage. The name of that undertow is resentment.

Resentments are the emotional residue from unresolved arguments, misunderstandings, injuries, attacks, and excessive conflicts. Although the damage from any particular incident may be small, the residue tends to accumulate over time, like plaque getting deposited on our arteries from too many fatty meals. The work equivalent to a heart attack is a sudden hostile episode, a "this time you've gone too far, especially after all that I've had to put up with from you in the past" event. Alternatively, a worker may just quit one day, never explaining that they're leaving because of a buildup of resentments over unresolved disputes.

Resentments can be almost as difficult to get rid of as arterial plaque. But, take heart: Resentment doesn't have to be surgically removed. Instead, those who are full of resentments need to find ways to think about their situations in a different way. If not, those resentments can build into hatred, at which point the relationship may be completely beyond repair.

There are basically two ways you can go about letting go of resentments. The first is to take the time and energy to work out your differences with the persons you resent. The message you must give to yourself in this case is "I have some unfinished business with ____. Rather than sitting here stewing about it, I'm going to talk with him/her about it. Maybe we can reach a new understanding. After all, he/she's not a bad person. It's time to clear the air." Notice that you have to go into the new discussion with a certain amount of hope, and with an attitude that the past doesn't determine the present. You also must be willing to use all the tools already mentioned in this book, especially trying to keep an open mind, really listening to the other's perspective, and keeping the focus upon the problem rather than the person.

It's usually best to speak directly to the person you resent if there's any realistic possibility of resolving your differences. However, sometimes you can't go directly to the other person. Perhaps the most common reason is that you already have tried several times to resolve these issues without success and so it no longer feels useful to take direct action. Another reason would be that you might get into trouble with that person or others if you did. A third is that you're resentful about situations beyond anybody's control, so that there is no single person to address. A fourth reason would be that you don't think you could stay in control of your words or actions. In that case you might say or do something that would only increase tension.

If you have resentments and cannot at this time take direct action then you must talk with the only person left: Yourself. You need to take stock of how these resentments are harming you. What are they doing to your body? To your mind? To your capacity for joy? Have your resentments taken over your being so that you're spending way too much time brooding about what people have done to you? Have you become obsessed with thinking of ways to get back at your tormentors? "Yes" answers to these questions indicate that you have indeed gotten caught in the resentment undertow and are being swept out to sea.

Fortunately, you can throw yourself a life preserver before you drown in that ocean of rage. The name on that preserver is "Acceptance." The basic idea is to recognize that most resentments build up around the idea that we are the victim of some particularly terrible fate because of what others have done to us. "Why did this happen to me, a good and innocent person?" seems to be the thought that rests at the center of resentments. But the concept of acceptance challenges that viewpoint. Acceptance begins with a realization that bad things happen to everybody in this less-than-perfect universe. Furthermore, there will always be someone out there who does things in exactly the ways that most bother you. That can't be helped. That's just the way the world works. Also, the past is the past and can never be altered. In addition, it usually helps to realize that we too cause harm to others that could lead others to resent us, if they so choose. Last, it's important to realize that the person who holds onto a resentment steals their own contentment and makes their own life miserable.

Acceptance involves making a determined decision to let go of the resentments you've been carrying. No more self-pity. No more brooding. No more obsessing. Instead, a powerful commitment to get on with your life, to grab your life preserver, and then to step completely out of that ocean of hate. Acceptance means letting go of the idea that others owe you anything right now such as an apology, a raise, or a promotion. However, acceptance doesn't mean becoming completely passive. You still have a right to fight for what you believe and want. Acceptance is primarily a way to deal with the world as is it, not as you wish it were.

The goal of this chapter has been to help the reader learn ways to contain their anger and reduce conflict in situations where some disagreement cannot be completely prevented. The four main ways to do so are by keeping your body calm, your mind open, your actions reasonable, and to look for the good in others. These behaviors on your part pave the way for the next concern— actually resolving conflicts as they occur. That is the subject of the next chapter.

4

Conflict Resolution

The Need for Conflict Resolution

Penny Hanks and Sandy Westby are good friends who've both applied for the same promotion. Only one of them can get it. They're both concerned about how this will affect their relationship.

✦

It's been a bad year, so the budget's been cut at Smith Electronics. But who will take the hit? Research and Development? Sales? Middle management? Everybody? The decision will be made next week at the executive council meeting. All the department heads are gearing up to protect their people.

✦

Norene Jacobson is upset. The only woman on a road construction crew, she's learned to be tough and to ignore a lot of harassment. But one man, Hal Carson, won't let up. Norene's decided she must directly confront Hal and insist he quit making improper remarks.

✦

Most workers dislike conflict. Conflict is stressful, distracting, bothersome, and exhausting. Conflict can bring out the worst in people—another good reason to avoid it, whenever possible. Nevertheless, some conflicts must be faced. People simply have different goals, values, interests, and ways of doing things. While it may be possible to accept many differences and at least tolerate others, sometimes one person's desire to go east directly contradicts another's wish to head west. That produces a situation in which nobody will go anywhere until the differences between these two are addressed.

The purpose of this chapter is to show you how conflict can be resolved in a productive manner. "Productive" here means several things: to clarify the initial problem in ways that make solutions possible; to get to the heart of the matter if there are unstated deeper issues; to find mutually beneficial solutions to problems that everybody can endorse; to end a conflict so that it doesn't keep coming up again and again; to maintain an atmosphere of respect before, during, and after the conflict is addressed.

This chapter is divided into three sections. First comes a discussion of how to prepare for conflict. Then you'll learn some effective communication techniques: positive ways to state your ideas, listen to others, and respond. The third unit deals with solution-seeking actions—on how to find mutually satisfactory answers to apparently unanswerable questions.

Preparing to Face Conflict

Alison Preston and Charlie Morgan designed a reading-improvement program together. They've named it "Funread," and it works really well for elementary school kids. Now Alison wants to copyright the program and market it to relatively wealthy school districts. Charlie wants to put the unrestricted program on the Internet so that all school districts can use it freely. They're stuck now, unable to proceed until they figure out what to do about this disagreement. They've worked well together so far, and this is the first time they've really disagreed about anything. Neither Alison and Charlie want to ruin their relationship, but both feel strongly about their position. They've agreed to meet in two days to try to resolve the matter. The question here is how they will use this time to prepare for this unintended and disturbing conflict.

Preparation for conflict can be divided into two main segments. The first involves people looking carefully at the core assumptions and attitudes they have about people in conflict. Next comes an awareness of how they and others deal with anger and conflict.

The Importance of Core Assumptions and Attitudes

Alison Preston headed to the local bookstore after work on Monday. She went straight to the business section hoping to find a book that might help her get through this conflict. At first she was discouraged because it seemed that most of the books on display had titles like *How to Manipulate Terrible People*, *Total Victory or Total Defeat*, and *How to Be a Lion Among Lambs*. The attitude of the authors was apparent in their titles: Everybody else, even your colleagues and coworkers, are merely pawns to push around the great chessboard of life. "I don't want these books," Alison thought. "They'll only make me angry and aggressive. Besides, Charlie isn't my enemy, and he isn't a pawn. He's someone I respect whom I happen to disagree with."

Alison, like many others in her situation, is searching for a set of good-faith principles that will help her enter into conflict optimistically and respectfully. Some of these are listed below:

Good Faith Workplace Conflict Principles

1. Although conflict at work may be uncomfortable, it often produces positive results when handled well—better results than if the conflict were ignored or avoided.

2. People who disagree can still respect each other.

3. Both you and the other participants in this conflict desire mutually positive results. Nobody is intentionally trying to destroy or harm others.

4. Each person in a conflict can help create an atmosphere of hope, trust, respect, and safety for all.

5. There is something worth listening for in the other person's position—a grain of truth that adds to your own ideas and positions.

6. An attitude of openness toward others—putting your "no" on the shelf—enhances the likelihood for effective problem solving.

7. Conflict is an opportunity to develop personal integrity: a chance to think carefully about one's deepest wants, needs, and values.

8. The final product of well-handled workplace conflict may be the mutual creation of a slightly better shared environment.

Conflict Can Yield Positive Results

Charlie Morgan hadn't anticipated having a serious disagreement with Alison Preston about marketing Funread. The truth is they never expected to take Funread past the testing stage. What a surprise when the results of the testing showed they'd hit upon some very effective new ways to encourage kids to read. They'd solved one problem—how to get kids to like reading. But every solution creates new problems, in this case what to do next with the program. Charlie's first instincts were to make Funread available for everyone. Alison's were to copyright and sell it for profit.

Unfortunately, Charlie hated disagreements. He'd come from an angry family where people fought constantly and never settled anything. His initial attitude toward conflict was usually to run and hide. But he realized he couldn't run away this time. He had to try to work things out with Alison. He also recognized that first he needed to change his attitude toward conflict so that he didn't think of it only as something terrible and useless.

The first good-faith belief about workplace conflict is that when well handled, it can do more good than harm. This doesn't make disagreement pleasurable, of course. Few people relish either the idea of discord or the process it takes to resolve conflicts. However, an overly negative attitude toward conflict is counterproductive. Conflicts are simply a fact of life. They are neither intrinsically good or bad. They just *are*. The fact that conflict occurs is a neutral event. The results of conflict can be positive or negative, depending a lot upon what attitudes people bring into their disagreements. Since so much of life is a self-fulfilling prophecy, coming into conflict thinking only of failure leads directly to failure. On the other hand, starting the process of conflict with the belief that it will lead to something good points the way toward success.

Note, though, the phrase handled well? in the first good faith principle. That's where each person in the conflict must take personal responsibility to create positive solutions. Conflict doesn't automatically produce good results. That only happens when the participants in a conflict make an effort to treat each other respectfully.

People Who Disagree Can Still Respect Each Other

All out, "kill or be killed" conflict creates intolerable stress. Conflict must be structured and limited for it to be useful. Otherwise, it can destroy a workplace, family, or country. That's why it's a tradition in many amateur and professional sports for the participants to shake hands before or after their encounter. The intent of the handshake is to remind each player to respect and honor the opponent. The adversary is an equal, someone worthy of appreciation. The goal of healthy competition is to defeat one's opponents, not to destroy them.

The word "respect" comes from Latin and literally means to look back or look again. What a great reminder during times of conflict, to look again at the person with whom you disagree, to make yourself see the goodness and value of that individual just when it's so easy to concentrate upon what you don't like about them.

Mutual respect is a vital part of controlling workplace conflict. Without respect, relationships quickly deteriorate into total hostility or complete avoidance. With respect, people can safely disagree with each other. Discussions will stay on topic and not disintegrate into personality attacks and screaming matches.

Preparing for conflict in good faith includes reminding yourself to respect the people with whom you disagree. They aren't evil or monstrous. They're just people. You need to remember to listen carefully to what they say, pass up chances to insult, attack or criticize, and look for things to appreciate in their ideas and personalities. Hopefully, they'll be doing the same for you. But, even if they don't, you'll be doing something valuable that will reduce your level of discomfort. You'll be treating the people in your workplace with respect and in turn helping yourself to feel self-respect.

Both Sides in a Conflict Want Positive Results

One goal in preparing for conflict is to reduce anxiety and fear. A good way to do this is by assuming that everybody involved in the disagreement desires a mutually beneficial outcome.

Conflicts can bring out people's hidden paranoid fears. That's when you start believing the first thing your opponents do in the morning is gleefully to rub their hands together while thinking of all the ways they can make your life miserable. "We'll start by losing his supplies. Then we'll tell the boss it's all his fault. Then we'll all laugh at his haircut and then . . . " In the midst of conflict you can forget that most people are far too busy with their own lives to be wasting their time trying to ruin yours. But it's not just that others don't have the time. They also don't have the desire to spoil your life. Few people are that mean-spirited.

I firmly believe that most people prefer "win-win" solutions in conflict situations. Sure, they hope to get what they want. Who doesn't? But they also want others to be satisfied as well. For one thing, human beings tend to feel better when they're with people who also feel good. For another, from a practical perspective it's best in the long run when everybody comes out of a disagreement feeling successful. That will cut down on the number of future conflicts and also increase the probability that those conflicts will produce mutually beneficial results.

I also believe that "win-win" solutions can be found for most conflicts. The process of seeking those solutions will be discussed later in this chapter.

Each Person in a Conflict Can Contribute to a Positive Atmosphere

Conflict resolution is often as much about process as content. The main process question is, how will the conflict be handled? That is where positive, good faith preparation can be very helpful. This kind of preparation involves visualizing the future in a particularly useful manner.

Alison Preston, for example, can imagine two very different scenarios as she prepares for Wednesday's meeting with Charlie Morgan. In one, the two of them greet each other cordially, spread out their work so they can sit side by side, express their appreciation of each other, keep their voices calm, and work toward mutually beneficial results. In the other scene Alison envisions two people stiffly greeting each other as if they were strangers, sitting on opposite sides of the table, criticizing each other's goals and values, raising their voices, and leaving the meeting just as stalemated as before.

What you see (in your mind) is often what you get. So, if Alison wants to increase the possibility for success, she could play the positive scenario out several times in her head over the next couple of days. Most importantly, by doing that she is empowering herself, taking personal responsibility for her share of the meeting atmosphere. True, she can't know for certain what mood Charlie will be in during the meeting. But that's not the issue right now. The only person Alison needs to think about at this time is herself.

The goal is to create a mutually hopeful, trusting, respectful and safe place. A sense of safety is especially critical for conflict resolution. Without it, people become defensive, pulling back into their shells for protection. One essential question to ask, then, is this: What can I do personally to help everybody in this conflict (including myself) feel more safe?

Look for the Truth in the Other's Position

People in conflict have a tendency to polarize their thinking: I'm right and you're wrong; I'm smart and you're dumb; I know everything and you know nothing. But real life usually isn't that way. Instead, each person in a dispute has a particular viewpoint that has at least a little wisdom in it. After all, your coworkers are probably almost as smart and motivated as you. They see things differently because almost everything can be seen in many different ways.

You might not know during the preparation phase what others see or why they think the way they do. You may only be able to get that information directly from them when you meet face to face. On the other hand, perhaps all you have to do is remember what they've already said. The main idea is to be willing to take in their viewpoint.

Rather than dismissing their ideas as totally absurd, commit yourself to seeking whatever value there is in them. Look for the grains of truth that are almost certainly present even in what you believe is mostly a mountain of chaff. It's especially difficult to seek value like this when there's been a history of ill will between workers. That's when most people want only to look for what's wrong with the other's position simply because it comes from that particular individual. But a notion that "If Joe wants this, it must be bad," is an example of biased and unproductive thinking. Positive preparation for conflict involves reminding yourself of your biases and making a personal commitment not only to bypass them but also to fairly evaluate what everybody else is saying while seeking the best mutual solution.

Adapting an Attitude of Openness Toward Others

"Yes" and "no" are two of the most important words in the English language. Both are needed to help us connect with others, establish boundaries, learn what we want, and make choices. Life goes best for most people when there is an even balance between one's "yesses" and "nos." Unfortunately, conflict seems to skew people quickly toward the word "no." No, I won't do things your way. No, that's all wrong. No, I'm sure your wrong. No, no, no, no, no. That natural tendency toward negativity creates a harmful atmosphere in which each person closes his or her mind and takes increasingly rigid stances.

Imagine, instead, that just before you enter into a conflictual discussion you metaphorically take your "no" and put it on a shelf. Then you can go into that conversation with a more open mind. You can start off with more of a "yes" attitude toward the problem and the people you're meeting.

This metaphor is particularly useful for people who are habitually critical, cynical, sarcastic, or pessimistic. Indeed, these individuals may have to look around awhile on that shelf even to locate their "yes," which could have more than a little dust on it from habitual underuse. But almost everybody can benefit from remembering to put their "no" on the shelf in conflictual situations. Besides, it will be waiting right outside the room, if you really need it. Try not to retrieve it too quickly, though, because once that "no" gets going, it tends to shove the "yes" right back on the shelf.

Conflict Is an Opportunity to Develop Personal Integrity

Our values operate at a subconscious level most of the time. We do so many things out of habit that we usually don't ponder the question "why?" But conflict often makes people think about their values because conflict frequently reflects disagreement at the level of values. That's why Charlie Morgan is doing some soul searching as he prepares for his meeting with Alison Preston. He is thinking carefully about what he's wanting from Funread. Why does he feel so strongly that they should give the program away on the Internet? Charlie eventually traces his thinking back to his high school social studies teacher Henry Jackson. Mr. Jackson's favorite phrase was that we all owe something to the world, a debt that must be repaid with generosity toward others. Funread is Charlie's opportunity to honor Mr. Jackson's teachings.

Values are complex. Our minds are full of value-laden rules and guidelines such as "Honor thy father and mother," and "Do unto others as you would have them do unto you." Values may have exceptions built into them: "Don't kill—unless you are defending your loved ones from attack." We may even have seemingly contradictory values that somehow manage to coexist in our brains and actions: "Be kind and generous," and "Strive for victory by defeating others." In addition, values frequently operate as a hierarchy with the highest value the one we are likely to honor if there's a conflict between them. For example, Charlie Morgan believes both in the value of getting ahead through personal initiative and in following Mr. Jackson's mandate to be generous to others. It's just that Mr. Jackson's guideline means more to Charlie than personal success. Giving Funread away would reflect his belief that generosity toward others is a higher ranking value than personal achievement.

Personal integrity demands more than just recognizing one's values, though. There's also the matter of living by them. It would mean little, for instance, if Charlie Morgan *said* he valued generosity more than personal success while quickly patenting his product and contracting with marketers to sell it. The measure of one's real values are in actions rather than words. Thus, some of the questions that workplace conflict can help clarify are: What are my most important workplace values? What actions am I prepared to take to remain true to these values? What am I willing to fight for? What values do I have that I would even risk my job to defend?

Value Ranking

Here, in alphabetical order, are twelve values that could apply in the workplace. How would you personally rank-order them, using the following guidelines: a) number one on the list is your most important value; b) if you had to choose between any two values you would usually select the higher ranking value; c) no ties allowed—force yourself to choose even if two values seem almost equal in importance; d) you may want to add or substitute a value not on the list if I have left off a particularly important one for you.

Value	Your Ranking
Achievement	_____
Aggressiveness	_____
Competitiveness	_____
Equality	_____
Fairness	_____
Financial success	_____
Friendship	_____
Harmony	_____
Honesty	_____
Partnership	_____
Power	_____
Security	_____

Conflict Can Create a Better Shared Environment

The general climate at work develops over time and is the product of thousands of communications among the organization's members. Disagreements, disputes, and other conflicts usually represent a small but significant proportion of those interactions. Each conflict contributes to how much satisfaction or dissatisfaction people feel.

Well-handled conflicts do more than settle problems. They help each participant feel better about themselves and the organization. They encourage feelings of competence and confidence. They also help develop shared commitment and a stronger sense of community. The final result of well-handled conflict are thoughts like these: "We did it. We sat down and talked through our differences. We took everybody's ideas into consideration and came up with a good solution. Nobody ended up feeling ignored or abused. In fact, everybody came out of that disagreement feeling respected and appreciated."

Occasional conflicts are a normal part of any organization's structure. Well-handled conflict helps people feel more optimistic about their organization. It makes them likely to deal more honestly and openly with others. Well-handled conflict also helps people believe that they are working together like a team rather than as opponents. Seeing that past conflicts have been settled amicably, they develop faith that future conflicts will also work out well. Thus, well-handled workplace conflict actually contributes to the mutual creation of a stronger, more resilient, and more effective shared environment.

Gaining Awareness of Your Conflict Style

Positive preparation for conflict involves more than developing a positive attitude toward conflict. It's equally critical to be aware of both your own and others' typical styles of handling conflict, since not everybody deals with conflict in the same manner. Indeed, each individual has their own unique patterns.

There are many different ways to describe conflict styles. One very popular way is to divide people into the categories of passive, assertive, and aggressive (Alberti and Emmons, 1986). Another model, well-known in the business sector, is based on the work of Kenneth W. Thomas and Ralph Kilman. These authors describe five major conflict styles based upon how people handle both assertiveness and cooperation. Very competitive people rate high on assertiveness and low on cooperation. Avoiders rate low on both assertiveness and cooperation. Accommodaters give in a lot because they overvalue cooperation at the expense of assertiveness. Compromisers balance their needs with those of others, always striving for "middle ground" solutions in which all participants get part of what they want. Finally, collaborators attempt to find "win-win" solutions in which all parties get what they most want. While each person may have a habitual preference for one approach to conflict, people who can use all five styles have the most flexibility. These people can fight strongly on behalf of their bottom-line issues (aggressiveness), ignore some issues that might take too much effort to bother with (avoidance), give in on some other disputes in the name of harmony (accommodation), bargain effectively as needed (compromise), and take the time to search for the best mutual solutions on the most important issues (collaboration).

In my own work I've developed a model of ten different unproductive ways in which people characteristically handle anger and conflict. Each of the ten conflict styles described below decrease the probability of resolving conflicts efficiently and amicably. It's important that you identify any of these patterns that affect you before you actually meet with others. Then you can guard against getting caught up in these ineffective methods of conflict resolution.

The Conflict Avoider

Conflict avoiders think conflict is a terrible thing that only brings trouble. They've often grown up in homes where conflict was considered morally bad, dangerous, or useless. They try never to get angry at work, and they get really nervous when people disagree. Conflict avoiders may also be accommodaters, giving in to more angry or aggressive coworkers in order to keep the peace. Many conflict avoiders have trouble setting boundaries with their colleagues because they cannot say "no" to them.

Conflict avoiders forget that anger and conflict can be useful. Usually conflict is a signal that something needs attention. It's like the flashing lights at a railroad crossing. But conflict avoiders sometimes close their eyes so they don't have to see the lights. They try to ignore conflict when they really should be attending to it. Conflict avoiders need to learn to speak up more often, to deal directly with important conflicts, and above all, not to feel afraid or bad simply because they happen to disagree with another.

The Passive Aggressor

"Don't get mad, get sneaky," is the theme song of the passive-aggressive worker. Passive aggressors seldom come right out and admit they're angry or in conflict with their coworkers. Instead, they adapt various indirect ways to tell others they are upset or to disagree with them. Some of these ways include forgetting to finish a job, showing up late to start work or for important meetings, literally falling asleep on the job, agreeing to do something but repeatedly failing to do it, disagreeing but only giving vague reasons for their position, and coming to work inebriated or drug affected. The basic message of the passive aggressor is this: "I don't like what's going on here, but I'm not going to tell you why. I also don't like you to tell me what to do, but I won't acknowledge that either. I'll just make life miserable for you by not doing the things you most need from me." The coworkers and employers of passive aggressive people often become extremely frustrated as they try to relate to them. The usual result of their efforts is to come away feeling as if they were pushing against a bowl of Jell-O: there's nothing to grab onto, no matter how hard they shove.

Passive aggressors need a positive agenda. They need to focus upon what they want, as opposed to quietly sabotaging others' goals. They must learn both how to say "no" to others and "yes" to their ideas. They need to work at cooperating with their colleagues, managing direct conflict.

The Overly Suspicious Worker

"What are they trying to do to me now?" is what overly suspicious people think to themselves. Untrusting, they stay on their guard all the time at work, trying to protect themselves against attacks from coworkers, supervisors, and customers. Overly suspicious workers tend to be loners because of their distrust of almost everyone in their world. They may appear paranoid to others, because they are so certain that even normal interactions are full of sinister implications. This excessively distrustful attitude makes conflict resolution difficult. How can any issues be settled when you're convinced that the people you're talking with are out to get you?

Overly suspicious workers need to decide to listen to their coworkers a little more and to expect problems less often. They need to stick to the issues at hand instead of looking for underlying plots against them. Mostly, they just need to learn how to trust. They must understand that trusting others is a choice we make that, in the long run, usually pays off in terms of greater mutual gain. Trusting others is not naive. On the contrary, it's a sensible way to cooperate unless and until there is clear reason not to trust.

The Sudden Exploder

You never know what's going to happen next with Harry Thompson. Harry's got a short fuse. One minute he's fine, but the next he's yelling, throwing his tools, and going ballistic. His anger doesn't usually last long, but it's sure long remembered by his coworkers. Harry says that's just the way he is. He's always had a tendency to become instantly furious when things go wrong or when somebody says something he doesn't like.

Sudden exploders are intimidators. The message they give is, "I'm a loose cannon, so you'd better not mess with me." Sometimes exploders scare others into giving them what they want. But frequently, exploders increase conflict rather than resolve it. The people they blast may become resentful, or they may get angry themselves and counterattack.

Sudden exploders need first to take responsibility for their actions. That means refusing to excuse their inappropriate behavior by saying they can't help it. Instead, they need to make a commitment to refrain from exploding, no matter what the immediate provocation. They also can learn to take brief time-outs when they sense imminent loss of control. "Think first, sit down, and keep quiet" might be a good motto for workers who want to gain more control over explosive anger.

The Conflict Creator

Most workers dislike and avoid conflict when they can. Not so conflict creators. These people seem to enjoy conflict. They feel right at home in the midst of disagreement. Sometimes they even try to stir things up just for the excitement. They like the strong feeling, the adrenaline rush, that accompanies conflict. While many conflict creators pick fights so they can personally experience that intense rush, others play the game a little differently. They prefer to get others fighting amongst themselves. Then they act like the audience for a wrestling match, cheering, jeering, and demanding more action.

Conflict creators may argue that they do so only in the name of a greater good, that conflict helps the organization function more effectively. They may even say they don't much like conflict itself, only the results of conflict. However, these rationalizations don't really describe their behavior or motivation very well. The truth is that conflict creators get bored when there's no good fight going on. In addition, they're not particularly interested in resolving conflicts. Indeed, they're often the people least able to sit down and reach compromises. Ending the fight stops the excitement, and excitement is what they're seeking.

If you suspect you may be a conflict creator (even once in a while) you may want to ask yourself these questions: Do I ever look for reasons to get angry or stay mad? Do I get a kick out of getting into arguments with my coworkers? Do I feel a little disappointed when a disagreement or conflict is finally settled? If so, you're probably contributing to useless and damaging hostilities. You may want to think about changing your attitude toward conflict, seeing it as something that's neutral and occasionally necessary rather than something that's always good.

The Bully

Unlike the conflict creator, bullies don't want conflict. They want compliance. They just expect and demand that others do what they want. Workplace bullies handle disputes through aggression. "Do it my way or else" is their motto. They often fly into rages to scare others into compliance with their wishes. Bullies may threaten, destroy objects, or even physically assault. Mostly, though, they attack verbally, insulting and demeaning anybody who dares cross them.

Bullies have learned a simple lesson in life: Intimidation often works. You really can get what you want a lot of the time by attacking others until they back down. What they fail to realize is that these tactics frequently produce short-term gains at the cost of long-term losses. The victims of such attacks deeply resent being bullied and they begin looking for ways to get even. Bullies gradually become more and more isolated, until they find themselves isolated and evicted from power.

Nobody wants to admit they're a bully. But if you see yourself in the description above you'll need to be honest with yourself. You'll also have to learn how to negotiate instead of intimidate and to treat others with respect.

The Thin-Skinned Worker

Fragile. Oversensitive to criticism. Easily hurt. Defensive. Insecure. Ashamed. Unconfident. These words describe people who use another ineffective way of dealing with conflict. They are so thin-skinned that they cannot handle normal and routine conflicts and criticisms. The message they give to others is this: "I'm sensitive. I need special treatment. Don't criticize me or I'll fall apart." When they do feel criticized, often by things that aren't meant as criticism, they may cry and look devastated, or they may counterattack aggressively, trying to hurt others as much as they feel they've been damaged.

Do you see yourself in this description? Then you need to start growing a thicker skin. Instead of expecting others to treat you like a delicate sculpture, too fragile to touch, you need to redefine yourself as strong enough for normal wear and tear. If self-esteem is a real problem for you then perhaps you'll need to adapt an "as if" attitude: Act as if you have good self-esteem until you actually develop it. Meanwhile, you may want to get professional help to help you think better of yourself so you can better handle conflictual situations.

One warning here: Just because your coworkers say you're oversensitive to criticism doesn't make it true. Sometimes others are undersensitive to their own habits of criticism and shaming. If you're not sure, you may want to consult with neutral parties outside the immediate battle zone, such as a trusted and fair coworker, the

Human Relations staff at your company, or an Employee Assistance counselor.

The Habitual Complainer

There's always something wrong in the world of the habitual complainer. Maybe it's that the break room is too far down the hall. Perhaps the paychecks should have been given out on Monday instead of Tuesday or the last shift should have fixed that broken lathe before they went home. Sometimes habitual complainers do notice a real problem that seriously needs attention. Often, though, they seem to be criticizing for the sake of criticizing. Their working day simply revolves around complaints. Their daily routine seems to consist of an endless pattern of grouching, grumbling, and grousing.

Anger, grouchiness, and complaining can become routine. But the price of being habitually grumpy is high. Personally, it leads to pessimism and depression. Interpersonally, it means perpetually going from one conflict to another. Habitual complainers can change, though. To do so they must make a commitment to focus upon the good in situations instead of the bad. They also have to learn to turn down a lot of opportunities to become upset with others because, frankly, there are always reasons to get angry if you look for them. In other words, they must choose regularly not to fight and instead to get along with others in a positive manner.

The Moral Crusader

Billie Nielson always seems to be fighting for a cause. The causes are often worthwhile, things like cleaning up pollutants and getting more lights in the parking lot. The problem is that she antagonizes people with her high and mighty approach. Billie frequently takes an "I'm better than you" stance. She acts as if she knows more than anyone else and that she's the only one with moral principles. Billie is contemptuous of others. She's always right and good; they're always wrong and bad.

Crusading like this creates enemies. Other workers naturally resent the crusader's self-righteous attitude. Conflicts are hard enough to settle between equals. It's a lot harder when one or both parties think that they are morally better than the other. Crusaders need to climb down from their soapboxes and quit acting superior.

They must realize that their coworkers are just as good as they are, even when disagreements arise.

Grudge Holders

Holding on to resentments is a major obstacle to conflict resolution. Resentments create an "I never forgive and I never forget" situation that locks people into rigid positions. Coworkers who have done you wrong then become implacable enemies. They must be defeated, humiliated, destroyed, beaten. Conflicts turn into grudge matches, with each side vowing to get even with the other for all their past injuries.

The best way to deal with resentments is to prevent them in the first place by addressing and resolving issues as they arise. However, that's not always possible. Sometimes things go wrong and feelings are hurt. That's when resentments begin to grow. Left to their own devices, these resentments can build, eventually turning into hate. Grudge holders only see the bad in those they despise. Whatever present problems or conflicts exist will seldom be resolved when people are this antagonistic to each other.

People let go of grudges in different ways. For some people, forgiveness is the antidote for resentment and hate. It's certainly not easy to forgive, though. Sometimes it may feel impossible. And yet forgiveness may be necessary to get on with one's life and work. The key to forgiving is not to simply forget about things but to make a commitment to let the past be in the past. You must choose to remember what happened without triggering your anger. For others letting go is a quiet process, a simple decision to get on with one's life. "I've spent enough time being mad at those people. It just makes working with them harder. So from now on I'll treat them like everyone else."

Effective Communication Techniques

Alison Preston and Charlie Morgan have done their preparations. They've each considered their positions carefully. They've committed themselves to negotiating in good faith. Also, each has identified their characteristic conflict styles. Charlie Morgan tends toward conflict avoidance and passive aggression. He'll have to be very careful to be assertive and not sneaky during this conflict. Alison Preston tends to be thin-skinned and explosive. She'll need to stay calm and not get defensive. Now it's time for their meeting, which they've arranged to take place in a quiet, neutral setting where there won't be any distractions.

Three processes must occur in order for people to communicate effectively with each other during conflict. First, each individual has to be able clearly to state their ideas, goals, wants, and needs. Second, each person must listen carefully to what the other is saying. Third, all parties have to be able to respond respectfully to each other's statements. Together, these three processes create a positive-feedback loop, an ascending spiral that increases the chances for successfully resolving an issue. But, without any one of these three, the attempt to resolve the conflict will probably only make things worse.

Being Direct, Specific, and Tactful

Charlie Morgan is a "hinter." It's hard for him to tell people directly what's really on his mind. Instead, he'll hesitate, hem and haw, or sound vaguely troubled. He hopes others will get his hints and realize something's wrong without him having to say it to their face. Indeed, it took Alison several weeks before she realized Charlie didn't want to market Funread for profit. She's still not sure why. It's in Charlie's best interest to communicate more effectively than that. He can do so by being direct, specific, and tactful.

Direct

Most workplace conflicts aren't chess matches. They aren't complicated conspiracies, either. They're simply disagreements about how best to proceed with some task or routine. There's usually nothing to gain by withholding information. It's better by far just to tell people exactly what you want and need.

Specific

Being direct involves saying what you want, while being specific adds "how." Specificity adds necessary detail to the picture. For instance, Charlie speaks directly when he tells Alison that he wants to give away Funread over the Internet. He adds specificity by suggesting they do so by renouncing their copyright and actively contacting school systems over the next year to inform them about the program.

Tactful

It's important to ask yourself one question before saying anything: How can I be direct and specific without coming across as rude or crude? Of course, we can't be totally in control of how others will respond. But we *can* use common sense to avoid saying things in ways that can easily be perceived as insulting. One way is to use the "I" statement format already described in chapter 2. "I" statements help all participants deal with conflict functionally with emphasis upon how one person's behavior affects another's.

Being tactful doesn't mean you have to walk on eggshells. Most people are strong enough to handle a little criticism or disagreement. Remember, though, that you are responsible for every word that comes out of your mouth. It's far better to say things politely the first time than to have to deal with the consequences of needlessly thoughtless, insulting, rude, or crude remarks.

Active Listening: How to Listen and Really Hear

Charlie Morgan is telling Alison Preston why he wants to give Funread away. He's talking about his great respect for his high school teacher Mr. Jackson, the man who taught him about generosity. His words are passionate. Unfortunately, Alison can hardly hear them. Her brain is so full of thoughts, worries, and wishes that she can barely listen to him.

Active listening is seldom simple. It's so easy to be distracted by external events such as the television at home or the telephone at work. One of the main rules for active listening is always to minimize the number of distractions. But the real problem in active listening isn't what takes place on the outside. It's what's going on inside one's brain that presents the greatest challenge. How can you quiet one's inner uproar long enough really to hear what others are saying?

Here are some guidelines to help you listen well during a conflict, even when someone says things that totally differ from your ideas:

- Focus on the conversation, putting everything else in your mind on hold.

- Make no assumptions about what the other person thinks, feels, or wants.

- Don't spend time rehearsing what you're planning to say while the other person is speaking.

- Let the other person have their say. Don't interrupt.

- Listen for feelings as well as thoughts.

- Notice the other person's nonverbal as well as verbal behavior.

- Demonstrate nonverbal attentiveness.

- Use active listening responses such as clarifying, restating, paraphrasing, reflecting, and summarizing to bring out the other person's wants and needs.

- Ask questions designed to gather information rather than to criticize.

- Be patient. Make sure you understand the problem as completely as possible before offering solutions.

Focus on the Conversation Exclusively

Right now, nothing else matters. Not where to have lunch. Not what to do next. Not even how to get what you want. The secret to good listening is to banish every possible distraction from your mind. That person sitting across from you is the only person in the world. The only goal is to pay such excellent attention that you will learn what's important to them.

There's a difference, by the way, between listening like this and simply appearing to listen. For example, a salesperson may seem to be giving a customer absolute attention while really concentrating upon only one thing: What do I need to say or do to make this sale? Only you, the apparent listener, knows the truth. But the difference between manipulation and active listening is huge. The person who simply fakes good listening won't learn what the other person wants and needs while the true listener will.

Make No Assumptions

People are predictable, but they're never 100 percent predictable. Nowhere is this more important to remember than when there is a disagreement. Conflicts can lock you into rigid assumptions about others' positions unless you are willing to look for the unexpected. It's vital to understand that your fellow workers are full of surprises. Just when you think you've figured them out, they will say or do something unexpected. No matter what someone has done or said in the past, it's critical to remember that they might not say or do exactly that same thing this time around. So make no assumptions. Instead, listen with an ear for the new and unexpected.

Don't Rehearse Instead of Listening

One certain way to miss hearing something important is to start thinking about what you want to say before the other person is half finished speaking. "Sure, sure, sure, yeah, yeah, I hear you—now will you just shut up so I can tell everybody my brilliant idea" is what people think while they rehearse their response instead of listening.

It's true that people think faster than they speak. That means a listener will always have thoughts running through their head while the other is speaking. But the kind of thoughts that are most helpful in listening are not "What can I say next?" but ones such as "What does she really mean?" "What is he feeling right now?" "What do they want and need?" These thoughts redirect one's energy toward better listening.

Don't Interrupt

Alison: What I'm trying to say is that we could ...

Charlie: I know, I know, we could make a ton of money.

Alison: Charlie, please quit mind reading. I was going to say we could certainly give Funread away to some organizations.

Charlie's an interrupter. He likes to finish other people's sentences. The trouble is that he often guesses wrong about what they're going to say. His habit of interrupting only gets everybody confused.

People interrupt for many reasons: Impatience ("I just can't wait for them to finish what they're saying. They seem to go forever"); status (workers with higher status tend to interrupt lower status workers); dominance (people try to show they are powerful by controlling the conversation); mind reading ("I know what they're going to say so I might as well say it first"); habit (some individuals simply picked up the habit of interrupting from their families and do so automatically). But whatever the reason, the effects are almost always negative. The interruptee's thoughts get cut off, perhaps never to get aired. That person may not say anything but will probably resent being interrupted. Interruptions convey the message that the interrupter doesn't value the ideas of the interruptee.

Of course it helps if speakers would remember to say their piece and then quit talking. It's hard not to interrupt someone going on and on or continually repeating the same words. Good speakers promote good listening just as much as good listeners promote good speaking.

Listen for Feelings and Thoughts

Conflicts are usually emotional events. That's because people don't just *believe* strongly in their ideas. They also *feel* strongly about them. It's almost impossible to advocate for what you want without experiencing moments of anger, frustration, sadness, and anxiety.

Imagine that the talker is transmitting information to you over your car radio. Instead of a control for right and left speakers, though, your radio has a dial labeled "Facts" and "Feelings." Some workers like facts so much they are tempted to completely turn the dial in that direction. Others are so fascinated with feelings they want to ignore facts. But that's like listening only to one speaker when you could have stereo. It would be wise to balance the dial so you could pick up the entire broadcast. If you only listen to facts, you won't be able to tell what's really important to the other person. If you only listen for feelings, you'll probably never get to problem resolution, since actual facts are needed to settle most issues.

Feelings aren't more important than facts. They're not less important either. They're part of the mix that a good listener hears and responds to.

Notice Nonverbal and Verbal Behavior

Just as your car radio has a knob for facts and feelings, it also could have a knob for "Verbal" and "Nonverbal" communication.

Again, the goal is to balance your awareness so that you're able to attend to both simultaneously.

You don't have to be an expert on nonverbal communication to notice that someone has their arms and legs crossed or that someone has shrunk into their chair so deeply they seem to take up no space or that another person's voice has risen in pitch and strength. Just be careful not to overinterpret these nonverbal signals. Sure, the guy with his arms crossed may be signaling that he's angry and unwilling to compromise. But, on the other hand, he may just be a little chilly. Let your awareness of the speaker's nonverbal communications help you understand what they're saying, but don't overemphasize that channel at the expense of verbal communication.

Demonstrate Nonverbal Attentiveness

Good listeners show the speaker nonverbally that they are listening. They do so by looking directly at the speaker, nodding their head (which often indicates "I hear you" rather than "I agree with you"), and occasionally saying noninterruptive comments such as "uh-huh." Again, the idea here is not to pretend you're listening by mastering a few tactics that merely convey the appearance of listening. The goal is to listen as well as you can, because the other person's thoughts and ideas are important.

Use Active Listening Techniques

Active listening is a process in which someone goes beyond simply taking in the other person's words. Instead, the goal is to help the speaker better develop their thoughts. Conflict can be resolved much more easily when people are able to state their ideas clearly, and that's exactly what active listening encourages. Active listening moves conversations from the general to the particular, from vagueness to specificity, and from the abstract to the concrete.

Clarifying is one active listening technique. Here the listener requests more detailed information. The basic message is this: "I'm interested in what you are saying and I'd like to learn more. Please fill me in." For instance, Alison mentioned that she would agree to give Funread away to a few organizations. Charlie may want to find out how many and which organizations she has in mind. All he has to do is ask her: "Alison, you said you would agree to give Funread away to selected organizations. Which were you thinking of?" This message acts to encourage the speaker to get more specific and detailed.

Restating simply involves the listener repeating back some of the words of the speaker. Thus, if Charlie Morgan says he's troubled about the way the world is becoming more and more materialistic, Alison could say, "So you're troubled by the materialism, right?" Normally, the speaker will make an emphatic affirmative nod and feel good that the listener is paying attention.

Paraphrasing goes beyond restating by putting the speaker's thoughts into slightly different words that still imply the same central thought or feeling. For example, Alison might try out "All the materialism really bothers you, doesn't it?" "Bothered" is a synonym for "troubled" but with a slightly less powerful tone. Charlie's response might still be a definite "Yes, I sure am." Or it might be "Bothered, that's an understatement. I'm outraged." Now Alison realizes she's underestimated the strength of Charlie's feelings. Paraphrasing like this tells the speaker two things: a) the listener is interested enough to think about the topic actively; and b) the listener wants to understand more about the speaker's thoughts and feelings.

Reflecting and *summarizing* are attempts by the listener to order and organize the flow of information coming from the speaker. After all, most people don't talk in a linear fashion. Instead, they start talking about one thing, drift to another, and perhaps eventually return to the first. Reflecting takes the form of zeroing in on one particularly important theme, the one the listener believes is central to the conversation: "Charlie, your commitment to your teacher's ideals seems really important to you, right?" The idea is to give the speaker a chance to return to that central concern or perhaps to correct your thinking: "Yes, but even more important is . . . "

Summarizing occurs after a longer conversation but not necessarily only at the end of a discussion. Alison would be summarizing if she said something like "Okay, so far you've mentioned two reasons you want to give away Funread—your dislike of materialism and your loyalty to your teacher. Do you have any other reasons?" Here the listener both informs the speaker that she's heard his main thoughts and simultaneously encourages him to continue.

Use Questions for Information, Not Criticism

Which of these questions is the most dangerous to ask: "Who?" "What?" "When?" "Where?" "How?" or "Why?" The answer, of course, is "Why?" because it may be meant either as a simple request for information or as a negative judgment. For instance, Alison might ask Charlie, "Why do you want to give Funread away?" She might mean just that, or she might mean "You idiot, what's wrong with you. Why would anyone in their right mind want to give Funread away?" But even if her question is perfectly well-intentioned, Charlie might think she's criticizing him. The moral of the story is to avoid asking "why" questions if you can. Concentrate on questions that will help make the conversation more specific. Alison might ask, "To whom do you want to give Funread away?" or "When would we do that?" Keep in mind, though, that any question can sound critical if you ask it with a sneer. It's not only *what* you say but *how* you say it that conveys interest rather than criticism.

Be Patient

How many times have you heard people say that the conflict they were having turned out to be a huge misunderstanding? One person thought the other believed something but then realized that wasn't the case at all. Impatience is one of the greatest sources of misunderstandings. Jumping too quickly into problem solving is one of the most common examples of impatience.

Conflicts, by their very nature, do need to be solved. However, they cannot be resolved effectively until people have taken the time to understand each others' central concerns. A crucial question for Alison to ask, then, is this: "Charlie, while you're talking I'd like to know if there's anything else important you could tell me about your wanting to give Funread away?" That one last question may well be answered with a "Well, there is one more thing I wasn't sure I wanted to mention, but . . ." Frequently, that one last item turns out to be the most important of all and the key to finding a mutually satisfactory solution to the conflict.

Effective Feedback: Responding vs. Reacting

Charlie Morgan has spoken his piece. Now it's Alison Preston's turn to give him some feedback. Charlie's hopeful that they can work things out quickly. But a look of disappointment crosses his face when he hears Alison's first few words: "Charlie, I get your point, but . . ."

Discussions involving conflict are difficult because they can so quickly spiral down into a series of attacks, criticisms, and insults. The standard form of these comments often begins "Well, yes, I hear what you're saying, but . . ." That single word—"but"—signals that the listener plans to reject what the speaker just said. It points the conversation directly toward confrontation, defensiveness, impasse, and stalemate. In "yes, but" feedback, the listener pushes against the speaker to defend a position rather than pulling with him or her toward a mutually positive solution. "Yes, but" feedback is more reactive than responsive, in that the listener defends against the speaker by instinctively pushing him or her away.

There are many variants of "yes, but" reacting. Here are a few:

- *Faint praise.* "Thanks, Sally, that was interesting. Next!"

- *Fault finding.* "You said it would cost us $110 million dollars to convert our system. But it really would take $112 million."

- *Shaming.* "That's one of the dumbest ideas I've heard around here in a long time."

- *Ignoring.* "Good idea, Joe—but we don't have time to bother with that today."

- *Dismissing.* "Yes, but we don't ever do it that way so there's no sense even thinking about your proposal."

- *Defending.* "What you say makes sense, Char, but I wish you packaging people would just concentrate on your stuff and leave us alone over here in production."

- *Diverting.* "Sure, Hector, but let's switch the subject of conversation to something else for a while. Maybe we'll get back to that later."

- *Logic attacks.* "Yeah, Joannie, but what you said doesn't make sense. You're not being logical."

"Yes, and" is a very different way to give feedback. While "yes, but" implies subtraction ("Let's dismiss this and this and this from what you said"), "yes, and" is additive ("Okay, let's start with your thoughts and keep going"). Speakers who receive "yes, and" responses usually feel both heard and appreciated. They, in turn, are more likely to listen to the responder's thoughts with a similar "yes, and" attitude.

There are several common forms of "yes, and" responses:

- *Approval.* "You know, Billie, that's an important idea. That's definitely part of what we need to do."

- *Good start.* "Tom, you've gotten us off to a good beginning. Now let's keep going and see what we can add to your ideas."

- *Selective positive attention.* "Anne, you've said several things here. Could we start with your idea to improve our rates of return mail? I agree that's something we definitely need to work on."

- *Logic agreement.* "That really makes sense to me. You've put a lot of thought into this."

- *Focusing upon mutual goals.* "After hearing you I realize that we have at least one shared goal. We both want to find ways to improve profit without laying anybody off."

- *Partial agreement.* "Of course we have some differences, Charlie. However, I certainly agree with you that we want to get Funread out to as many students as we can."

- *Willingness to seek positive solutions.* "Belle, this may take awhile. Let's schedule some time to get together so we can come up with a good solution to your concerns."

- *Willingness to be mutually creative.* "Marti, it looks like we're going to have to think of something really new to resolve our disagreement."

Every one of these responses conveys the message to speakers that their ideas are valued and respected. Almost certainly these "yes, and" responses will lead to less conflict and better problem solving. Because of that, you might think that everyone would use this kind of feedback frequently. Unfortunately, the reality is that "yes, and" responses seem to go against peoples' instincts during conflict. Most responders must consciously learn to make "yes, and" responses when their gut tells them to defend and attack with "yes, but" reactions. They have to train themselves to hear what's right in the other's ideas instead of what's wrong. The rewards for doing so, though, are certainly worth the effort.

Resolving Issues: Successful Negotiation

Alison Preston and Charlie Morgan have been talking for several hours. Now they're finally getting somewhere. They've agreed to begin marketing Funread for profit while also selectively donating the program to some of the nation's poorest school districts. Most important, they've discovered that their personal goals, which initially seemed hopelessly different, could both be achieved. They could make money *and* be generous with Funread. Better yet, they could stay friends and business partners.

Win-win resolutions like this are not always possible to achieve. However, they're more probable when all parties negotiate in good faith, respectfully, and competently. Negotiation is a skill that can and must be mastered in order to achieve positive solutions to conflicts, or what I call the "good enough" solution.

A good enough solution is one that respects the law of diminishing returns. That law postulates that there is a point in any effort where the amount of energy consumed in an activity exceeds the value gained from that activity. For example, a new gardener will learn perhaps a hundred good ideas by reading one good book on gardening. Then she might gather fifty more thoughts from the second book, twenty from the third, ten from the fourth, etc. Eventually, the gardener will know so much that reading another book on gardening may take more time than it's worth. The law of diminishing returns dictates then that she quit reading (or switch subject matter to a new but related topic such as freezing vegetables). The gardener has become "good enough." It would be a waste of time for her to try to become perfect.

So, what are the characteristics of good enough conflict resolutions?

First off, good enough solutions are ones in which the individuals involved stop damaging each other or the organization. My initial goal when facilitating conflict negotiation is always to get people to quit hurting each other. "Stop the worst first" is a useful motto in these negotiations. Do that, and then gradually work toward ensuring that all parties lay down their weapons and cease attacking each other. Practically speaking, this means that nobody is gossiping, sabotaging, undermining the other's efforts, squeezing others out of the action, storming ahead without regard for others, etc. Getting participants to quit harming each other helps focus everybody upon developing positive outcomes rather than defeating, damaging, or destroying each other.

Another characteristic of good enough solutions is that they resolve more problems than they create. Of course, every solution to a problem creates some new challenges. For instance, Charlie Morgan and Alison Preston will have to figure out now how they can balance making money with being generous. But some alleged solutions create far more problems than they resolve. Imagine, for instance, a businessman who decides that the way to deal with his time management problem is simply to quit sending out bills to his customers. True, he'll have more time for the rest of his business—but soon there won't be any business. At any rate, one extremely important question to ask before adopting any possible conflict resolution is this: "What new problems will this proposed resolution create?"

Third, the negotiated good enough solution must break any main impasses between the parties. Impasses are the "stuck points" that must be resolved and yet seem impossible to resolve. A good enough solution may not answer every concern, but the people involved will be able to say that they can at least go on now. The "both/and" process mentioned previously is very helpful in eliminating impasses. And, because the impasse is broken, good enough agreements permit immediate, observable success. "Great," Charlie and Alison say as they conclude their talk, "now we can start marketing Funread right away."

Immediate success is not sufficient, though. Good enough solutions must also point toward future directions. This means that the participants won't soon have to return to negotiating. Instead they'll be able to use their energies for more immediately productive activities. This is important because conflict resolution usually consumes a great amount of time and effort. Who wants to make that kind of investment only to have to return to the negotiating table next week?

The fifth marker of a good enough solution is that everybody gets something important out of it. This characteristic returns us to the concept of always searching for each party's underlying interests. What's really important to them? What central wants and needs are masked beneath each party's position on a specific issue? Good enough solutions speak to those central needs. Only when those interests are addressed will people say things like "I didn't get everything I wanted, but I can live with this agreement." Compromise and collaboration are the mechanical processes that allow each person's central interests to be successfully addressed.

Finally, good enough solutions must past the goodwill test. Have the participants generally emerged from their negotiations feeling mutually respected? Are they optimistic about the prospects for this specific project? Do they also feel positive about the process of working with each other? If not, more harm than good may have been done, despite the appearance of a satisfactory outcome. It's critical to remember that conflict resolution is more process than content. The question here is how positive that process has been. If all has indeed gone well, then everyone should emerge from the good enough resolution feeling perhaps tired, even exhausted, but good about themselves and their colleagues.

The Problem-Solving Process

Mark Umbreit (1996) suggests a seven-stage problem-solving process that I find quite useful for conflict resolution. The steps are these:

1. Define the problem in terms of the desired state (the general, nonspecific goal).

2. Identify options for solution and clarify any options that are ambiguous (brainstorm).

3. Evaluate alternative solutions.

4. Decide on an acceptable solution.

5. Develop an implementation/action plan.

6. Develop a process for evaluating the results.

7. Talk about the experience.

This approach to problem solving is clear and straightforward. Furthermore, it defuses especially emotional situations by helping all parties discover a mutually beneficial resolution to their differences.

Perhaps the hardest step in this process is the first one, defining problems in terms of a desired state. This doesn't mean coming up with a final solution, though. Rather, the goal is to set the stage for negotiations by imagining what a generally positive solution would entail. With Funread, for instance, Charlie and Alison might agree that a positive outcome would allow them to know how, when, and in which ways they could bring their program to school systems. This understanding, in principle, about what they want to achieve, allows them to get on to the specifics of negotiating their differences regarding implementing that goal.

Umbreit's second stage is to identify and clarify options. This stage is often called *brainstorming*. The key to brainstorming is to generate as many possible ideas with regard to the goal while not permitting any criticism or judgment. Brainstorming sessions typically produce some suggestions that are practical ("We could call in a marketing specialist"), and some more whimsical ("We could ask all the third graders at our kids' schools to vote"). Occasionally, somebody will hit upon a really new and brilliant way to do something during one of these sessions. However, I believe that the real value of brainstorming is that it loosens people up, helping them break free from previously locked-in beliefs and positions.

When Alison and Charlie brainstormed, they thought up over twenty possible solutions, ranging from the practical (agreeing to give away their product to the poorer communities; marketing Funread for profit, but setting up a related nonprofit corporation) to the impractical (destroying the program in the name of friendship; selling it to the first half of the alphabet and giving it away to the other half).

Evaluation of the possibilities and making a decision are the next two steps. Which choices are feasible? Desirable? Relatively satisfactory to all? In line with people's (and the organization's) goals, hopes, wants, needs, and values? Are there any true "win-win" solutions available? If not, what kind of compromises can be made to maximize mutual gain and minimize individual loss? Which choices would lead to the kind of good enough solution described earlier? The hardest aspect of this component is being fair and objective, as opposed to rigidly defending your original position. It takes courage to ask yourself what really will work best rather than how you can get everybody to do what you want.

Eventually, Alison and Charlie came up with three possible solutions that they could both live with: creating a community board to advise them on nonprofit operations; aggressively marketing for profit for two years, then donating the program to one hundred needy communities; and immediately giving away Funread to twenty communities and using them for one more year of testing. Charlie and Alison then evaluated each of these possible solutions based on several criteria: practicality; how quickly each would get the program into the marketplace; amount of time each would consume; how personally challenging each would be; and so on. They eventually decided to market Funread for profit over the next two years before giving it away. They came to this conclusion when they realized that trying to do both at the same time would take more time and energy than either wanted to spend. Charlie felt a little sad about the delay in delivering to the poorer communities, but concluded that Funread would only become more finely tuned over the next two years, and would therefore be even more useful when it did arrive in those communities.

Developing an action plan and the way you'll eventually evaluate the results means turning a theoretical decision into a practical game plan. Umbreit describes this stage succinctly with this question: "Who will do what by when?" Although this seems fairly clear, many negotiated solutions break down at this nuts-and-bolts stage. It's fair to say that almost nothing has been accomplished until "who will do what by when" has been specifically answered. Failure to make these decisions almost guarantees that the apparently resolved issue will soon return to haunt all the participants. Failure to develop a reasonable way to measure the implementation of the plan paves the way to future frustration and finger pointing.

In the case of Funread, Charlie agreed to develop a detailed marketing plan within three months, while Alison made final adjustments to the manuals that accompanied the program. Full implementation of their plan was scheduled to begin in January of the next year. They also broke up each general job into smaller sub-tasks, agreed upon dates for the completion of each, and agreed to meet every two weeks to evaluate their progress.

Finally, Umbreit suggests talking about the problem-solving experience before wrapping it up. Such discussion is helpful for two reasons: It provides a final check to see if anything important has been neglected; and it allows the participants to comment on the process of negotiating as well as the final resolution.

Conflict resolution takes time and energy. It's sure preferable to the alternative, though—conflict *nonresolution*. The cumulative effect of problems that are ignored or unresolved is the gradual decline into inefficiency, poor morale, and even business failure. On the other hand, successful conflict resolutions increase overall effectiveness, improve morale, and keep businesses competitive.

5

The Threat of Violence

A Scary Time at Work

Maggie Branch feels a little scared every day she has to go to work at the Powerlift Health Gym. Jim Fisher, one of her coworkers at the gym, has been making veiled sexual remarks for several weeks. Maggie's ignored them as best she could, as well as his uncomfortably lingering stares. It doesn't help that Jim's name was in the paper recently after he was arrested on a domestic violence charge. But Jim's not the only person Maggie fears. She's also scared of her boss, the formidable Vanessa Powers, a six-foot-tall former model known for her "Do what I tell you to do *now*" attitude. Ms. Powers doesn't get angry all the time, but you'd better get out of the way when she does. She's fired excellent workers more than once for insubordination when all they were doing was trying to discuss an issue with her.

Maggie is confused as well as scared. She's mentioned her concerns to a couple of coworkers, Belinda Carlson and Mike Knight. Carlson, who works a lot with Jim Fisher, says he's always been polite and appropriate with her. She thinks maybe Maggie's just imagining the whole thing. Knight, on the other hand, says he's heard Jim say a few times that Maggie's really sexy but stuck up. He suggests that Maggie stay away from Jim. As for Ms. Powers, they both agree that Maggie has every right to be scared. They are too. A few days ago, in fact, Mike thought he was going to get canned simply because he suggested buying a few new pieces of equipment. "It's sure no fun working here anymore," he adds. "Not when you have to be on your guard every minute."

Jim Fisher, the object of Maggie's fears, is a very unhappy man. Not only is he having a lot of trouble at home (his wife recently threw him out and got a restraining order against him), but he's so broke that he's considering filing for bankruptcy. Regarding Maggie Branch, Jim's really beginning to dislike her intensely. Every time he talks with Maggie she only gives him brief answers and quickly goes away. As far as he's concerned, Maggie's one of those nose-in-the-air women who make him feel dumb and worthless. Sexy but aloof. Tantalizing but unavailable. Women like Maggie get under his skin. That's when he begins making not so subtle remarks designed to make them feel as uncomfortable about him as he feels toward them.

More and more discussion has taken place over the last several years about the concept of a "hostile workplace." What's become clear is that many behaviors can contribute to making one's workplace feel scary and inimical. Threatening behavior ranges from the crude (physical or sexual attacks) to the subtle (veiled threats, ambiguous remarks). Intimidating behaviors may be gender, race, nationality, or religiously focused. They may be intentional or unintentional. The overall result of these words and actions is that the targeted individual feels scared. Indeed, one good definition of hostile workplace behavior is any action that causes a reasonable fear or intimidation of others, whether or not that behavior is intended to intimidate. What makes an action hostile, then, is partly in the behavior itself and partly in the mind of the recipient of that action. The commonsense test is to ask if most reasonable and objective witnesses to the act would consider any particular behavior or a series of actions intimidating. If so, that behavior or set of actions would be considered hostile.

However, my concern here is more broad than with only those actions that would formally be considered hostile. Rather, I'm interested in the ramifications of a very common scenario: Sometimes things start to go wrong between two or more people and they just keep getting worse. Anger builds up. Resentments grow. After a while a permanent rift develops within the office or work area. Coworkers become enemies who must be fought or guarded against at every encounter. Military analogies then pretty accurately describe the workplace atmosphere: the fog of war, a state of siege, guerilla warfare, a battle of attrition. People come to work in full battle regalia, complete with weapons (figurative and literal) to use against their enemies and armor to protect against the other's attacks. Workers who get caught up in these wars go through their days feeling scared and angry. They often go home tense or exhausted.

Physical safety can definitely become a concern in these situations. Fistfights are not uncommon, especially between men. Homicidal attacks are even possible (homicide is the leading cause of death at work for women employees, although many of these deaths result from estranged spouses who attack their partners or former partners at their workplace or from random assaults by outsiders). Most frequently, however, workers attack each other with words. Damage is measured in terms of bruised feelings, lowered self-esteem, diminished work performance, increased rates of absenteeism and health problems, and accelerated staff turnover. The cost of these fights is enormous at both the individual and organizational levels. Everyone suffers when anger and hostility begin to dominate the workplace.

It's invaluable to understand the dynamic process that occurs during the development of these long-term animosities. This process is the subject of the next section of this chapter. From there we'll turn to the characteristic warning signs for possible workplace violence and then to discussing how individuals can respond effectively to intimidation and assault. I'll also describe how management can help protect their workers. Finally, I'll suggest tips on how to deal with angry supervisors, bosses, and owners.

Hostility and Violence Progressions

Hostility is basically an attitude one person or group takes against another in which the second person or group is labeled as essentially bad, evil, or dangerous. Hostility itself is neither the emotion of anger nor a physical act of aggression. Instead, hostility is a mental predisposition, an extremely negative set of beliefs and attitudes. Hostility is almost always the end product of a long series of unsatisfying interactions between two persons, although often only one of the people becomes hostile. The exception to this generalization is in the area of prejudice. Deeply biased individuals may be hostile toward people they've never met simply because these people are members of a particular group.

From Hostility to Hate

Hate is the end product of hostility. Hate is a feeling of extreme aversion toward another. People who hate have grown to despise and detest each other, even to loathe being in each other's presence. Hate, when present in the workplace, turns offices into outposts from hell and production areas into seething battlefields.

Hate usually develops slowly. It often begins with a single bothersome issue between two people that doesn't gets resolved. Jim Fisher, for example, began disliking Maggie Branch one day when he brought some mail in to her and she failed to acknowledge him because she was on the phone. Jim characteristically didn't say anything to Maggie but instead filed the incident away in the personal-grievance section of his brain. From then on, he began noticing other times when Maggie seemed to ignore or dismiss him. Still, he said nothing to her, although he did mutter a few nasty comments about Maggie to his coworkers. This pattern of paying selective attention only to what someone else is doing wrong constitutes the second major step in the development of hate.

The anger that accompanies unresolved issues often gradually solidifies into resentments. Resenters believe they have been intentionally wounded by the other person. Jim Fisher at Powerlift is sure that Maggie Branch didn't just happen not to notice him. Oh no. She saw him standing there but chose to ignore him. Resenters believe they are the victims of another's animosity toward them. They usually fail to notice how they may be contributing to the problem, or if they do know what they're doing, they defend and justify their actions as necessary responses to the other's aggression. Jim Fisher, for instance, recognizes that his increasingly nasty remarks and looks are making things worse, but he tells others he only makes them because Maggie keeps ignoring him.

Resentments are bad enough. However, the hostility train sometimes keeps going right past that stop and continues on to "Hate," the next station along the tracks. The greatest difference between the two is that people who hate each other see almost no possibility for reconciliation. Hate feels like a permanent situation. The anger that began to solidify as resentment has now hardened into the mental equivalent of concrete. As Jim Fisher begins to hate Maggie Branch his thoughts focus on how she "always treats me like I'm lower than a worm." That word "always" is a sure sign Jim is moving into hate. After all, people who "always" or "never" do something cannot change. Because Jim believes Maggie will always treat him contemptuously, he can validate his increasing hatred toward her.

The hostility train has even one more station past hate, though. The name of that final stop is "Revenge." People getting off here spend lots of time fantasizing how they can get back at the persons or groups they hate. Sometimes they go past fantasy into aggression. At work such hostility-based actions may take such forms as physical assault, sabotaging the other person's work, rumor spreading, and trying to get the other person in trouble or fired. Once again, perpetrators feel justified in taking these actions because they think they're merely retaliating against others who have purposely elected to hurt them.

The Four Pathways of Hostility

One important piece of information about hostility is that it almost always follows a course of increasing breadth, moving along four main pathways. First, hostility moves from the specific to the general. Second, it travels from one individual toward more persons and groups. Third, it moves from the present into both the past and future. Fourth, and most ominously, hostility travels a path that takes people from seeing each other as human to seeing them as simultaneously subhuman and superhuman.

The Specific to the General

Let's begin with the movement from the specific to the general. Work resentments usually grow like ice building up one layer at a time during an ice storm. Each negative episode constitutes one such layer. And, just as dozens of these layers can eventually become so heavy as to break off the branch, so will dozens of unsettled conflicts, poorly worded memos, and unfortunate misunderstandings lead to a severed relationship. Adding to this process is the tendency that already upset people have to quit noticing any positive interactions that might counteract the negative ones.

From the Individual to the Group

Hostility also travels from the one to the many. One reason for this is the natural tendency people have to try to convince others that they are in the right. Jim Fisher, increasingly bothered by Maggie Branch's behaviors and attitude toward him, soon tells anyone at work who will listen about her faults. He'd like the others to take his side. Meanwhile, Maggie may be doing the same as she also attempts to collect sympathetic colleagues.

Another way hostility travels from the one to the many is through guilt by association. Jim Fisher may extend his antipathy, for instance, to Maggie's close associates, her work crew, women who look like her, or even to all women. Notice how any one person's actual behavior becomes less and less relevant as this process develops. Eventually hostility frees itself almost completely from real behavior and takes on mythic proportions. Hostility becomes more or less "free floating" as it expands: free from actual behavior, free from rational control, free from efforts to contain it.

Spanning Time

Resentments that produce hostility expand in a third alarming manner. They move from the present into the past and future. The key phrases here, spoken or thought, are these: "Now that I think about it, I realize they've done this kind of stuff to me before" and "I'm sure this isn't over yet. They'll keep trying to hurt me." This particular expansion adds to people's feelings of hopelessness. Nothing will change because it's been going on so long and will certainly continue indefinitely into the future.

Dehumanization

Finally, people become dehumanized as angry resentments become true hatreds. Oddly, the objects of one's hate become both less than and more than human. They become subhuman in the hater's mind because they are perceived as evil and monstrous, beneath contempt and unworthy of respect. Simultaneously they are feared for their alleged strange power over their supposed victims. It's almost as if the hated parties could magically interfere at any time with one's life and work. Imagine how hard it is to resolve conflicts or even to speak reasonably with others who are looked upon with so much fear and hate.

Workplace Aggression

Resentments are bad enough when they are limited to people thinking bad thoughts about each other and not enjoying working together. However, unresolved hostilities can also lead toward another progression, from passive thoughts to active aggression and violence. Workplace aggression is defined here as *any behavior, verbal or physical, that could or does cause harm to another worker's body, mind, workplace relationships, or job performance.* This definition includes such actions as intentional sabotage of another's project and malicious gossiping. Also, an act can be aggressive even when the perpetrator claims no conscious intent to harm such as by "playfully" shooting staples from a power stapler in another worker's direction. The key question is whether reasonable observers of these behaviors would agree that they *could* hurt or *have* hurt another worker.

Please see the Anger and Violence Ladder displayed on the next page to see how aggression can progress in the workplace.

Sneaky Anger and Aggression

Maggie Branch is getting upset with Jim Fisher's grumbling. She wants to get back at him but at the same time she doesn't want him to know his behavior is bothering her. "I know," she thinks to herself, "I'll just put off ordering those weight training machines he's been after. He won't be able to say a thing because it's not really my job to order them, but I know he assumes I will." Maggie's behavior is classified as sneaky aggression. She's hurting another worker by not doing something wanted, needed, or expected.

Sneaky anger is fairly common in the workplace, if only because it's a useful tactic for angry people to use against those with more authority or power. The classic worker slowdown or military game of exactly following the letter of the law instead of the real intent are both examples of sneaky anger. Probably the best way to prevent such tactics is for management to involve everybody as much as possible in the business. When all workers have a real investment in the organization's success, there is less tendency to sabotage the company's efforts through inactivity. In real-life practice, though, sneaky anger often permeates the workplace and significantly lowers productivity.

"You can't make me" is the motto of anger sneaks. These workers are masters at frustrating others through inactivity. They show their anger indirectly by forgetting to bring the right tools along on

The Anger and Violence Ladder

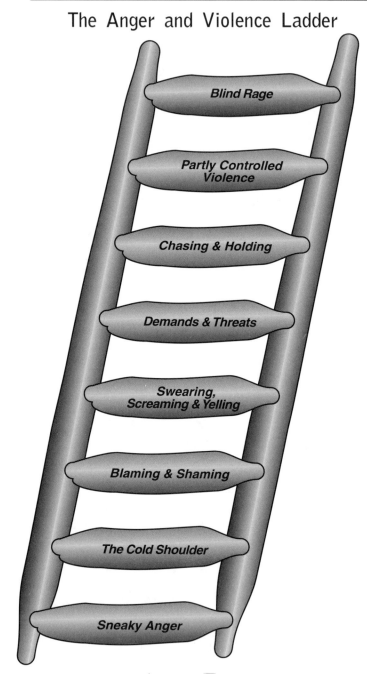

*From *Angry All The Time*, R. Potter-Efron, 1994, New Harbinger

the job, delaying important tasks, slowing down to a crawl at exactly the moment speed is essential to get a job done on time, playing dumb or helpless when they really know what to do, failing to keep promises they've made to other workers, quietly resisting authority often simply by ignoring orders, and using the phrase "yeah, but . . ." to argue against any and all direction.

Anger sneaks may or may not be consciously aware of their anger or how their passive resistance affects and frustrates their coworkers. They don't have to acknowledge their anger because their main weapon is doing nothing when they should be doing something. Indeed, when challenged about why things keep going wrong around them anger sneaks will often say they're not to blame because "I didn't do anything." The sad part is that they are exactly correct. It is their inactivity that negatively affects their colleagues.

The Cold Shoulder

Apparently Maggie Branch's sneak attack on Jim Fisher hasn't been very effective because Jim is still making insinuating remarks and bad-mouthing her to their coworkers. So now she decides upon a new tactic. This time she's going to ignore him completely. She'll not speak to him at all even if he says something directly to her. Maybe then he'll get the idea that he should leave her alone.

Ignoring. Silence. Coldness. The message is "I am angry with you, but I won't talk about it. Instead, I will treat you as if you don't exist. That will make you feel really bad. Consider my silence an act of punishment."

People at all ages need acknowledgment of their existence. Little acts like head nods, eye contact, and routine "How's the weather?" conversations are important in maintaining one's equilibrium, not to mention necessary task-oriented workplace communications. We take these interactions for granted until they quit happening. That's when most people realize how uncomfortable life can be when someone refuses to make contact with them.

The ancient practice of shunning took ignoring to an extreme by ordering all members of a community to have no contact at all with someone who offended them. But a sort of informal shunning can also occur at work when one or more individuals refuse to speak with others. One recent example was the reaction of union baseball players to the promotion of a few of the men who played for the owners during their long and inimical strike/lockout. Most team members were reported to be simply refusing to talk with these players for weeks or even months. Some of them apparently desired not only to punish these players with their silence but also to drive them off the team.

There's no question about the effectiveness of giving someone the cold shoulder. It works. However, this behavior almost certainly exacerbates an already difficult situation. People feel violated by another's grim silence. Besides, problem solving is impossible when coworkers aren't talking with one another. Giving others the silent treatment will very likely lead to increased animosity and even more contentious acts of aggression.

Blaming and Shaming

"Maggie Branch does not belong at Powerlift. She's totally incompetent. Her mistakes are costing the company a fortune. Besides, she's no athlete. Why should we have staff who can't outperform the customers? She's not good enough to work here." Jim Fisher's escalating his campaign against Maggie. He's trying to convince everybody that there's something so basically wrong about Maggie that she should be fired. He's blaming Maggie for the company's problems and shaming her by calling her a poor athlete.

Blaming and shaming are further acts of aggression. They convey five main messages in the workplace:

- You are no good.

- You are not good enough.

- You don't belong here.

- You're not wanted.

- You should go away.

These statements may be made directly to one's antagonist or, like Jim Fisher, to anybody and everybody who might listen. In either case the object is to embarrass, demean, and humiliate another worker, to cast them as incompetent and unworthy. These blaming and shaming attacks often lead to escalating blaming and shaming counterattacks. The end result of this pattern is a group of bitterly insulted people totally disrespectful of each other.

Swearing, Screaming, and Yelling

Vanessa Powers, the owner of Powerlift, is a yeller. Customers in the pool area can sometimes hear her screaming at her staff way back in her office. "My gosh," they say to each other, "what's wrong with that woman?" Several persons have even canceled their club memberships because Vanessa's yelling bothered them so much. Ms. Powers can also swear a blue streak when she chooses. Unfortunately, she chooses to do so just about every day.

Most organizations, especially production facilities, tolerate a certain amount of cursing and yelling. Most of the time such actions are considered to be harmless ventilation. But it's important to recognize that swearing, screaming, and yelling are very invasive verbal behaviors. Short of constantly wearing sound protectors in one's ears it's virtually impossible to shut these noises out even if they are not aimed directly at you. And it's normal to feel threatened and attacked when you're the recipient of someone's shouts or curses. Intended or not, these behaviors are frequently perceived as acts of aggression. Clearly, it's crucial that organizations limit the amount of screaming and yelling that goes on as well as giving strong messages that swearing at other employees (or customers) is unacceptable.

Swearing, screaming, and yelling are signs that people are losing control over their anger. If not confronted, either by themselves (screamers realizing on their own that they're in trouble and immediately taking steps to cool down) or by their supervisors or concerned coworkers, this verbal aggression sets the stage for even more dangerous behavior.

Demands and Threats

Fuming, Maggie Branch marches into Jim Fisher's office. "Jim, I'm giving you a warning. If you don't quit harassing me, I'll make your life miserable around here. You'll regret ever bothering me, you two-bit loser."

Maggie may have a right to be angry, but right now she's doing everything wrong. First, she's let her emotions dominate her judgment. She knows the best thing she can do is to stay away from Jim Fisher but instead chooses to barge in to his office. Second, Maggie is not specific. Neither her complaint about being harassed nor her threat to make his life miserable is specific enough to do anything useful. Third, she's setting herself up to be labeled the problem at

Powerlift. She could easily be disciplined or even fired for this thoughtless act of aggression.

Do it, or else. That's the central message people make when they threaten each other. But, unless you are in a position of total power over the other, these demands usually spark an angry resistance. "Do it, or else" simply provokes "Oh yeah? Try to make me!" responses. Furthermore, making demands and threats often backfires, even for those with power, because the recipient may very well respond with passive aggression: "Yes, you can make me do this, but you can't make me do it well."

Demands and threats may be crude or subtle. One well-known, subtle form follows the theme of "Play along with me, if you want to get ahead in this business." Another is "Just do it our way and don't ask too many questions, okay?" No matter how obvious, though, the main idea is always the same—"do it my way or you will suffer."

Chasing and Holding

As the fight between Jim Fisher and Maggie Branch gets worse, people are getting alarmed. The latest story is that Jim suddenly appeared in the doorway of Maggie's office just as she was preparing to go home for the day. Jim made several nasty remarks about Maggie's work. He both glared and leered at her. Worst, though, was that he stood there in the doorway and wouldn't budge. Maggie had to ask him to get out of her way four times before he finally moved aside. She was definitely shaken by the incident. Now she's wondering if it's even safe for her to come to work.

Chasing and holding is one of the least understood areas of violence and aggression, whether such behavior takes place at home or in the workplace. It's also frequently excused and explained away rather than being treated as an act of aggression. But physical violence occurs whenever you take away someone else's choices, including using superior force to restrict another's freedom of movement. Grabbing someone's arm to make them listen, positioning oneself to prevent entry or exit, following somebody around without reason, refusing to leave when told to do so: all these and similar acts are aggressive in nature. Each unfairly restricts another's right to choose where to go, with whom to talk, and what to do. These kinds of actions must never be excused as innocent or meaningless because, in fact, they are violations in themselves and, if permitted without sanctions, may encourage other violent behaviors.

Partly Controlled Violence

Maggie Branch is intimidated by Jim Fisher, but she's also ashamed of feeling scared. She believes that, if you don't stand up to bullies their behavior just gets worse. But she doesn't know what to do. She's tried talking with management, but that hasn't helped. Vanessa Powers mostly shrugged and told Maggie to take care of things herself. So here's her plan: The next time Jim belittles her or makes a suggestive remark she's going to slap him right across that big mouth of his. Today she's going to tell her friends at Powerlift about her plan so they can witness the encounter and back her up.

Partly controlled violence is the next step up The Anger and Violence Ladder. It's controlled because the aggressor is attacking another person with a purpose in mind. The goal is to make someone else do what you want or stop doing something you dislike. People don't completely lose their head in these situations. Actually their violence is planned and contained. There's a big difference, for example, between Maggie's slapping Jim and her bringing a gun to kill him.

Still, the phrase "controlled violence" is pretty much an oxymoron, a self-contradictory statement. Violence can never be completely controlled or contained. Think, for instance, of the number of boxers who've died in the ring despite the use of gloves and the presence of referees. Violence is like a caged tiger snarling at its keeper, waiting for an opportunity to strike. That's why I use the phrase "partially controlled violence" to describe this kind of goal-directed aggression. There's always a risk that what begins as apparently controlled violence can rapidly spin out of control.

Blind Rage

"My God! What's got into Jim? He's going crazy. We better call the cops!" Jim Fisher came in today angry at the world. Then his pal, Marco Wells, made a sarcastic remark about Jim still being hot for Maggie Branch. A strange look suddenly came into Jim's eyes. He grabbed Marco and threw him to the floor, shouting something nobody could understand. Now he's tearing up the gym with his bare hands, screaming about not taking any more crap from anyone. Vanessa Powers has told Maggie to get out of the place immediately before Jim goes after her. Everybody's scared, and nobody knows what to do.

Blind rage is the last step up The Anger and Violence Ladder. This rage is like a church organ being played as loudly as possible with all the stops removed: the result is lots of chaotic noise but no coherent music. During blind rages people might attack others or themselves. They might destroy any objects in sight, their own as well as others. Sometimes they fall into a trance-like state so that later they won't remember what they did. This relatively rare condition happens when the "new brain" is overwhelmed by the anger pouring out from the older parts of the brain, in particular the limbic system that is the source of our emotions. The new brain, whose job it is to control that anger, shuts down much like a circuit breaker disconnects one's electrical system to prevent total overload. The only goal of someone in a blind rage is to survive by attacking and destroying whatever or whomever is in the way. Kill or be killed. That's why it's so dangerous.

The anger and violence ladder may also be viewed profitably as a pyramid. The great majority of aggressive interactions take place at the base of the pyramid (sneaky anger, cold shoulder, blaming and shaming), the fewest at the tip (partly controlled violence and blind rage). That's why direct communication without judgment is so helpful in curtailing potential violence at lower levels of hostility—because workers can still listen and respond to each other then. However, direct communication probably won't work by the time people have begun threatening, holding, and physically attacking each other. By then, intermediaries may be needed to cool the participants down and to preserve safety in the workplace.

Who Is Likely to Be a Threat

Hostility is fundamentally a long-term mind-set that turns immediate anger into an overarching negative attitude. Hostile persons transform "I'm angry with you right now" into "I'm permanently angry with you." This means that the capacity for hostility is as universal as the capacity for anger. Hostility, as described above, could occur in almost any workplace between almost any people under certain circumstances. Furthermore, the same idea applies to the potential for physical aggression. Just as any parent is capable of physical violence toward their children during periods of tremendous stress, so is any worker capable of physical violence against another worker, if things go badly enough over a long enough period.

Violence is indeed a fairly common problem within the workplace. One study from 1993 concluded that two million employees were physically attacked at work in the year ending July 1993, while another listed the deaths of over one thousand employees as cases of workplace homicide. Indeed, homicide is the leading cause of workplace death for women and the second leading cause of workplace death for men (Myers, 1994). Although it is possible to exaggerate concern (since the great majority of workers don't ever experience threats ever in their careers, and also because some of this violence represents overflow from domestic disputes), still it is reasonable to conclude at this time that workplace violence and the threat of violence are significant problems.

Over time, a profile of workers who are most likely to become violent has emerged. Frequently described characteristics include:

- male

- thirty to forty years old

- a loner

- obsessed with guns

- with a history of violence

- hostile toward authority

- defensive when receiving criticism

- job means everything (I am = what I do)

- alcohol or drug abuse

A history of aggression appears to be the best predictor of violence among these indicators. However, it must be emphasized that predicting violence is much more difficult than simply looking for people who fit this profile. This is true for two reasons. First, many workers who match this profile will never act dangerously toward others. Second, as noted previously, even unlikely candidates for aggression could conceivably become violent if pressed too hard and too long.

Donald Myers (1994) divides the causes of workplace violence into long- and short-term factors. Long-term causes include stress, personal problems, economic conditions, employment conditions, and social or political causes or beliefs. Stress often develops in the workplace over role conflicts, relationship problems, and neglect of one's health. Common personal problems are alcohol abuse, compulsive gambling, emotional or mental problems, financial worries, and legal difficulties. Economic conditions include the financial solvency of the employing company, the state of the broader economy, and the risk of layoffs. Employment conditions that can add to the threat of violence include a poor fit between the nature of the job and the worker's needs (for instance a repetitive job performed by a worker who craves variety), exhausting or stressful work conditions, and harassment from other workers. Finally, some people may condone violence at work because of their beliefs or values, perhaps justifying an act of aggression in the name of their religion, political beliefs, or philosophy.

Myers notes four short-term conditions that could lead to workplace violence. These are discharges from employment, disciplinary actions, layoffs or job abolishment, and disagreements between and among coworkers. He comments that "People do not like to hear bad news; they dread hearing devastating news," such as company downsizing decisions and employment discharges.

Could You Be Violent?

Could you be a candidate for workplace violence? The only way to answer that question is to be as honest as possible with yourself. One question to ask is in which ways, if any, do you fit the profile of a potentially violent person as described above? Other important questions to ponder: How much stress have you been in over the last several months? How stressful is your current situation, both at work and outside of work? Are there any signs that you're becoming increasingly angry or aggressive at work? Are you quite concerned about losing your job? How well do you handle criticism? How do you respond to authority? Are you becoming increasingly frustrated about anything or with anyone at work? If so, what can you do to alleviate your frustrations? Have any of your coworkers told you that you need to calm down, take life easier, not take offense so easily, and so on? Do other workers seem scared of you even though you don't understand why? Are you overdoing your use of alcohol or any mood-altering substance? Do you feel more anxious or depressed than usual? Have you been coming on a little too strong lately? Have you developed a "hair trigger" temper, blowing up quickly and sometimes without a clear cause? Are you scared that you're close to losing control and doing something stupid?

While no single answer to any one of these questions is definitive you may be heading toward an episode of workplace if you're responses indicate that you are becoming increasingly violence prone.

Responding to a Coworker's Anger

Each episode of anger and aggression is unique. That means an effective response to any act will depend upon the particulars of that situation. The only absolute rule is this: *Safety first.* The top priority of the responder to another's aggression must be to protect their own safety, the safety of other employees, and even the safety of the aggressor. Physical safety always takes precedence over problem resolution. This risk factor also helps determine the responder's action. Naturally, the response to another's anger and aggression partly depends upon the severity of the behavior. While it makes good sense to sit and talk with a worker who is mildly upset or irritated, obviously that strategy would be worse than useless with someone shooting off a gun.

Remember that most people's anger is just that—anger. Only a small percentage of angry workers turn their anger into actual physical acts of aggression. Even those who are violent usually are so quite infrequently, although they may threaten others more often. It's easy to overestimate risk because of the defensive "flight or fight" response people normally have to being the object of another's anger. However, there is a big difference between a person's anger (an emotional state) and their aggression (physical behavior). Therefore, *any threats or acts of violence against you or a fellow worker must be taken seriously.* They should always be reported and documented carefully. No one should ever be expected to work as if nothing were wrong in the face of the threat of violence.

Looking back at The Anger and Violence Ladder, it's useful to divide that ladder into three basic levels of anger and aggression. The top layer consists of blind rage, party controlled violence, chasing and holding, and making threats or demands—all of which can be named the Attack Level. The middle range includes swearing, screaming, yelling, blaming and shaming, and is identified as the Intimidation Level. The relatively mild acts labeled cold shoulder and sneaky anger can be called the Annoyance Level. Your response to an act of aggression should be tailored to each level of risk.

Responses to Attack Level Aggression

Attack Level aggression involves a direct act or the threat of an act that causes harm to or curtails the freedom of movement of an employee. Someone in a blind rage, intent upon total destruction of people and property, is demonstrating the most extreme form of Attack Level aggression. Less extreme and more common are acts of partially controlled violence that are at least partly practical in nature—in other words, aggression intended to obtain a particular goal. I include chasing and holding behavior in this category, even if the behavior is not accompanied by any other show of force, because the victims of these actions are deprived of their right to privacy and choice of companionship during these episodes.

As noted above, protecting your personal safety should be your first goal when confronted with workplace aggression, especially Attack Level violence. There are several ways to protect yourself. For instance, it's always a good idea to get away from the aggressor, especially if that individual displays a weapon. This is certainly no time for personal heroics or "macho" tests. Rather, the goal is to avoid confrontation. The idea is to get out and call for help, if you can.

But what if you can't get away? Then the best you can do is to minimize the risk of getting hurt by acting in a nonthreatening manner. This means curtailing your urge to make threats, escalate the fight, or give orders that can't be immediately backed up. Instead, concentrate upon your nonverbal behavior. Keep your voice calm, relax your facial and body muscles, speak and move slowly. Do not walk toward the aggressor, since that action might be taken as a threat. It will also help to display relatively open body language, such as unfolding your arms instead of crossing them defensively. The goal is to demonstrate calmness in the face of threat. Remember that many aggressors, quite possibly including the person in front of you, are afraid when they're enraged (think of rage as a combination of furious anger and terror). That means anything you could do to lower the attacker's fearfulness might also lessen their aggression. Your calmness may send out a "no panic" message to the aggressor that will help relieve the need for further violence.

Your verbal messages should indicate calmness and self-control to the aggressor just as much as your nonverbal messages. Keep in mind that this is not the time for complex interactions, fancy words, abstract principles, and so on. Aggressive and especially enraged individuals usually can't understand anything but clear and simple messages. Keep your sentences brief and safety oriented. Try to get the violent individual to sit down, slow down, quiet down. If you can get through at all, attempt to ally with the person in the name of safety. The idea is to get the person to choose calmness themselves rather than impose it upon them: "Okay, I'm ready to stop now. I'm sorry I blew up," is the best possible result in these unfortunate circumstances. However, continue to use nonthreatening verbal and nonverbal interventions even when the person seems more calm. Otherwise you might accidentally trigger another burst of aggression. Don't be surprised if the person vacillates between attack and nonattack for a while as their body gradually becomes less aroused.

It never helps when the attacker is intoxicated. Indeed, it may be virtually impossible to communicate with a very drunk or high aggressor. Nevertheless, if you can't get away to a place of safety you must assume that the individual still has some ability to choose, no matter what appearances seem like. It's sometimes helpful to remind the attacker about their generally nonviolent values and ways of doing things ("Joe, I know you're a peaceful person") to forge a bridge between their inebriated and normal states of mind. Don't tell them that normally they're nice but right now they're drunk. Instead, keep the emphasis upon how they value staying calm and peaceful (by implication, even when they're drunk).

Attack Level violence is dangerous and scary. These incidents should never be ignored or forgotten after they're completed. The cost of doing so is sending messages to the aggressor that acts of violence are acceptable in the workplace and to the rest of the staff that their safety cannot be protected. Rather than that, attacks should be responded to at all company levels. Management must assume responsibility to enforce a nonviolence policy through appropriate punitive and nonpunitive interventions. Critical incident debriefing is also needed for the victims of and witnesses to workplace violence. Trained staff should be available to help these persons deal with what happened, how it affected them, and how they can get back to business as usual. It's particularly important after a violent episode for everyone to believe realistically, based upon the overall response to that event, that the probability for another act of aggression has been lessened and that attacks against employees won't be tolerated.

Responses to Intimidation Level Aggression

Intimidation Level aggression is behavior such as swearing, screaming, yelling, blaming, and shaming that is designed to frighten and bully others into doing what the aggressor wants. Some threats and demands also could be classified at this level (as opposed to Attack Level), in particular threats to get the targets of the threats into trouble at work or to make their lives miserable unless they do what is demanded. But aggressors gain more than just an immediate advantage through such behavior. Intimidation also establishes longer-term dominance. The intimidator, if successful, establishes a "better not mess with me" atmosphere that fosters both immediate compliance and avoidance of any actions that might displease the aggressor. Intimidation tactics may be pursued consciously by the aggressor, or the motives behind such behavior may be more unconscious. The main concern, however, is not the conscious intent but the actual effects of aggressor's actions. Intimidation occurs when reasonable members of an organization become scared by the words or actions of someone in the workplace.

The key to responding to these intimidation tactics is to remember that all workers deserve to be treated with respect. Being treated with respect means no name calling, put-downs, or humiliations. It means being listened to and taken seriously. It means sitting down and talking issues over calmly instead of being subjected to verbal attacks and threats. Your goal, whenever you're the target of intimidation tactics, must be to be treated respectfully. Although you may not be able to achieve this goal every time, aiming to be treated with respect consistently is the best way to improve what others say to you.

The general method of responding to Intimidation Level aggression has three parts: 1) declining as much as possible to participate in interactions that are intimidating; 2) inviting the intimidator to engage in positive problem-solving behavior once that individual curtails inappropriate behavior; 3) afterwards, assessing both your own behavior and the affects upon you of the incident.

Declining to Participate

The main lesson intimidators need to learn is that you will not give in to the intimidation (even if you're scared). Nor will you allow yourself to get caught up in destructive personality contests. It's better by far with an intimidator to model appropriate behavior, especially calmness and control, than either to give in because of fear or get sucked in to the fray through an angry, undignified response. This means that the best response to someone's yelling or shaming is often simply to ignore the behavior entirely. That nonresponse is certainly better most of the time than its alternatives: a defensive counterattack that plays right into the intimidator's hands; a guilty agreement that you've done something wrong; or placating the aggressor by doing what they want. Declining to participate in intimidating interactions ensures that if anybody makes an ass of themselves around the workplace it won't be you.

Inviting Positive Engagement

Frequently, the best one can hope for is to minimize and neutralize the negative effects of intimidators. However, sometimes it is possible to take the next step: to invite the aggressor to get down to the real business of resolving any tensions or problems between you. One way to do this is by selectively responding positively to any reasonable statements made by the intimidator while still ignoring their hostile comments. Imagine, for example, staring quietly and motionlessly at the attacker in the face of a blaming attack but then immediately nodding your head and responding to a more reasonable remark. Another method, more likely necessary when the intimidator will not refrain, is to tell them directly that you'll be happy to discuss their concerns as soon as they calm down and quit attacking. It's important here not to get drawn into an argument about whether or not their behavior is inappropriate, however. If the intimidator tries to move in that direction you'll have to just repeat your message and break off immediate contact. Also, don't accept responsibility for the aggressor's anger or actions. Remember that they are choosing to act that way and could choose to quit being so intimidating at any time.

Chances are pretty good that aggressors will gradually change their approach when they realize they're not getting what they want. That's when you may want to acknowledge their anger and their reasons for being upset. This, again, is an opportunity to pair effective problem solving with mutually respectful behavior. Basically, your offer is to help the other person turn their ineffective anger into more effective action as long as they continue to behave themselves.

Personal Review

Intimidators are emotionally draining to their targets. They sometimes tap a person's worst fears, shame, and anger. That's why it's important for you to take some time for personal review after dealing with someone's intimidation tactics. Questions to ask yourself include: What do you feel good about in this situation? What do you wish you'd done differently? What emotions did you feel? What thoughts helped or hurt you in handling this situation? What personal skills and strengths did you use? Do you need to talk with anyone about this? Do you need to ask for help from others (coworkers, management, friends, family) with this person? Is there anything you need to do so you can let go of this scene and get on with your job? What do you need to do for yourself or to get from others so you can feel safe?

Responding to Annoyance Level Aggression

Some shaming and blaming behavior is more annoying than intimidating. This is especially true when the aggressor is habitually critical or grumpy. These persons tend to shame and blame more to express their ego needs than in an effort to control. Their basic message is "I'm better than you." Their goal is to establish their superior status as against making others do something specific. Nevertheless, this behavior is still aggressive in that one individual is harming another. It's just that the main emotional weapon has been changed from fear to shame.

Refusing to speak or work with someone (giving someone the cold shoulder) is another Annoyance Level act of aggression. So is sneaky anger when it emerges as a refusal to help another worker or a shunning of one's appropriate responsibilities. Indeed, both of these tactics could endanger coworkers in some occupations. Imagine, for instance, an angry electrician who won't tell a coworker that a line he's working on is "hot." But even without physical danger, these acts of omission create many job problems such as the members of one department in a firm "forgetting" to pass along critical information about a business opportunity to the members of another department. Although it's easy to underestimate the cost of these behaviors (since they do feel like annoyances rather than major problems) they definitely cause a significant amount of disruption in the workplace.

Annoyance Level aggression should not be ignored in the same way as Intimidation Level aggression. Instead, it's important to address and confront Annoyance Level aggression immediately, as soon as a worker begins to use this weapon to attack. The goal is to deal with the worker's complaints before these tactics become entrenched. It's far better to risk an uncomfortable few minutes now than the prospect of having to deal with a cold war later.

Each type of Annoyance Level aggression can be handled through direct communication. The format for doing so with people who are refusing contact often goes like this: "Helen, I've noticed that you seem to be avoiding me. You haven't really said anything to me for a couple days. Is there anything going on that we need to talk about?" Note that the questioner is simply opening the door to the possibility for discussion rather than apologizing, taking responsibility for causing a problem, or accusing.

Annoyance Level shaming and blaming can also be directly addressed. The best approach here is a specific request/demand that the aggressor cease that behavior. As usual, it's best to phrase your request in workplace relevant language: "Bill, that's the third time today you've put me down in front of others by calling me weird. I don't like that at all. Besides, it's not helping us make this deal when the Smith people hear that. Don't make fun of me anymore."

Sneaky anger and aggression is always difficult to handle because the passive-aggressive person usually denies their anger: "What do you mean you think I'm mad at you? I'm not angry. I just couldn't get here on time." Still, you have nothing to lose by bringing the negative behavior to light. It's best to stay calm in these situations. Getting mad at a passive aggressor only plays into their "Why is everybody always mad at me?" life stance. Emphasize, if possible, how their unhelpful behavior affects them rather than you: "Tammy, I'm going to have to write you up for getting here late because it delayed our entire work crew. You'll have to talk to the boss about it." Don't expect any miracles here. Passive aggressors are as stubborn as a boulder. But ignoring their behavior never works and only breeds more sneaky anger.

How the Company Can Help

Before ending this chapter, I want to emphasize that increasing workplace safety is the responsibility of each individual within an organization but also of the organization itself. Below, I've presented some key methods that companies can use to address hostility, anger, and potential violence in the workplace.

Prevention is the first concern. What can an organization do to protect its workers from unnecessary danger? A good first step is to study general working conditions. Are the employees of the company working under highly stressful, dangerous, or unhealthy conditions? Are staffing levels high enough to prevent excessive pressure? Have there been in the past or are there now long-term stressors, such as the threat of layoffs or reorganization? Does management have a history of showing appropriate concern for their employees, or are they known for their cavalier attitude? In short, what is the company doing in general that deters or promotes feelings of anger, outrage, unjust treatment, fear, and so on? There is no question that workplace violence prevention begins at the top, with a firm commitment of the organization's leadership to disallow hostile and damaging behavior.

The next issue is that of the business' traditional practice regarding any and all forms of aggressive behavior. Is there, for example, a history of tolerance of abusive management? Is aggressive "fooling around" tolerated, even when it has led to injuries, arguments, or fights? Is racism or sexism implicitly permitted because of the inaction of management? Have bullies been allowed to dominate other workers? Is excessive verbal aggression encouraged in the name of healthy competition? Or has management made it clear in their disciplinary actions, promotions and demotions, and daily routines that acts of aggression are unacceptable and will not be tolerated?

Written policy comes next. All organizations need clearly stated policies that spell out the fact that workplace violence will not be tolerated at any level of the workplace. The goal in writing should be zero tolerance of any behaviors that might be dangerous, violent, threatening, or harassing. Any action that could reasonably be construed as hostile by the recipients of that behavior must be firmly prohibited, regardless of the stated intent of the initiator. General policies must also be combined with more detailed descriptions of how members of the organization should respond to any threats or actual incidents of violence. These guidelines are meant to provide usable information and protection to workers and managers who have to make difficult decisions when suddenly faced with emotionally arousing situations. They may prevent serious errors of judgment. Of course, these paper rules will only be useful if they're broadly distributed to the employees and when the leadership of the business emphasizes that these policies will be regularly enforced.

Organizations can help prevent violence by creating ongoing violence-prevention groups drafted from all work areas. These groups can be given several important responsibilities including providing their colleagues with information about safe and respectful treatment, responding to complaints and threats of violence, and promoting worker safety through violence prevention. These groups should receive special training themselves on the subject so that they will have both competence and skills if they are needed to step into a potentially violent situation. Their training should include learning how to help their coworkers deal with all three levels of aggression described previously in this chapter. They should also be activated whenever members of the organization face major stress, such as the possibility of a significant layoff or reorganization.

Finally, leaders of the organization must be sure that company personnel respond quickly and appropriately to the aftermath of any threatening or violent incident. Critical incident debriefing should be provided both to the participants, witnesses, and any other workers affected less directly by the incident. These debriefings, and the active participation of company leadership in them, provides visible evidence that the organization firmly and consistently advocates nonviolence in the workplace.

The Overly Aggressive Boss or Supervisor

This chapter is basically about the discomfort workers face when they must deal with their coworkers' anger, hostility, threats, and violence. Nowhere is this more evident than when the source of their concern is their immediate supervisor, their employer, or the owner of the firm. These people enjoy a power advantage over the worker that can never be ignored. While the anger of an employee can bother a boss, that boss' anger threatens the employee's career and financial survival. In addition, the very traits that often help people rise to the supervisory or ownership level—ambition, drive, control, impatience, perfectionism, energy—can lead to trouble. Supervisors and owners also must deal with the great stresses that come with greater responsibility, such as constant worry, time pressure, and fatigue. Given these factors, supervisors and management must nurture a special sense of discipline to remember not to abuse their position by intimidating their subordinates. Certainly it helps for them to remember that their behaviors and attitudes set the tone for the entire organization. If they are frequently angry, irritable, critical, violent, nasty or just plain mean they may very well end up dealing with a group of like-minded employees.

So what if you are the unfortunate target of a supervisor or owner's wrath? Is there anything you can do, short of printing up your résumé and getting out as soon as possible? I believe the answer is affirmative—within limits. In other words, yes, you can do things to lessen hostilities, but only so much. It's certainly unrealistic to think that any person in a subordinate status can completely alter their working environment. On the other hand, you probably can do some things that at least resist unfair treatment and promote mutually respectful communications. The best general approach is to follow the guidelines for dealing with Intimidation Level aggression, ignoring the person's intimidation tactics as much as you can while inviting more positive communication both verbally and nonverbally.

Two questions to ask yourself are these: "Does my boss know that he or she is being a jerk? Would it do any good to say something?" Remember that most people, even bosses, don't want to be labeled as terminally mean, and that they may not be aware of how their behavior is affecting you. If that is the situation, it might be worth the risk for you to speak up. People are much more likely to change their behavior when they realize that their actions are causing problems. As usual, keep the focus upon work and offer a positive alternative if you choose to speak directly to your supervisor: "It really distracts me from my job when you shout at me, Betty. My productivity goes down because I get so nervous. I think I'd get more done if you would speak to me more quietly."

What if your answer to these questions is that you believe your boss is fully aware and consciously choosing to intimidate? It might be wise then to ask others their opinion just in case you are in a definite minority position. Perhaps you've become defensive and have grossly overestimated that individual's meanness. However, if others validate your answers, then you probably should update your résumé. Who wants to work the rest of their career for a tyrant? In the meantime, avoid and ignore the bully as much as you can, quietly insist on being treated with respect whenever possible, gather a good support network to minimize the boss's effects upon your self-worth, and remember that you are neither the cause nor the solution of that person's behavior.

It may be helpful to talk to someone else in authority about your boss's intimidating or aggressive behavior. This approach will be most effective when others are also complaining and if the person you speak with has the ability to intervene usefully. If you choose to go this route, be sure to bring with you specific and clear examples of the behaviors that bother you. Since the person you speak with will almost certainly ask if you have tried speaking directly to your supervisor, you must be prepared with an answer—either a "Yes, but it didn't work. Here's what happened when I tried," or a "No, because I'm afraid I'll be attacked even more. Here's what happened the last time I (or a coworker) tried to talk with him or her."

A formal, written complaint is another possibility. This path is usually a next-to-last resort (the last resort being formal legal action) taken after a series of disrespectful behaviors and the breakdown of informal interventions. Taking this action announces that there is an ongoing problem and usually results in a very uncomfortable working environment. Nevertheless, it may be the only viable way to insist upon respectful treatment.

Taking on the boss is seldom easy and often risky. Only you can decide if it's worth it. Remember, though, that you do have a basic right to work in safety and freedom from intimidation.

6

Do You Have an Anger Problem?

The previous chapters of this book are intended for everybody. This chapter is designed especially for workers who believe they could have a serious problem with their own anger. They believe that either because others have told them so, or because they can tell something is wrong because of their frequently angry actions, feelings, and thoughts.

This chapter is written in a question and answer format. The questions asked are the ones I've heard frequently from these workers and sometimes from their coworkers and supervisors. I have also included questions people ask about how to handle other workers' anger and a few questions about anger in general.

Here is a list of the questions in this chapter to help you get to the ones you are most interested in:

1. Can't I ever get angry at work?

2. Why can't I just let off a little steam?

3. When is anger justified?

4. What's good about anger in the workplace?

5. How is my anger dangerous to my health?

6. Why can't I stop getting angry?

7. Are there any medicines to help me with my anger?

8. How can I make a commitment to be less angry?

9. Are there different issues for a woman who's angry at work?

10. How can I slow down my temper?

11. How can I accept criticism better?

12. What if I'm just being funny?

13. How can I be less critical of others?

14. How can I leave work stress and anger at work?

15. Will minimizing my anger decrease my power at work?

16. What are the rules for fair fighting?

17. How can I take a time-out when I can't physically leave?

18. Could I be covering up my real feelings with anger?

19. Why do my coworkers think I'm angry when I'm not?

20. How can I tolerate a particularly irritating person?

21. Will I take this anger to my *next* job?

22. Could my recent drinking and drugging be related to my work anger?

Questions from other workers about anger at work:

23. How can I avoid getting sucked into others' anger?

24. How can I tell my friend that he or she has an anger problem?

25. Should I resign if my workplace is too angry?

Can I Ever Get Angry at Work?

This question is usually framed as a complaint: "Everybody tells me I get too angry at work but certainly there must be some times when it's okay to get angry. After all, my coworkers do an awful lot of really stupid things. Do you expect me just to sit around and smile when they act like idiots?"

The answer to this question is that nobody can tell you never to get angry at work (or anywhere else, for that matter). That's up to you. But remember the concept of anger invitations. Every day each of us receives dozens of invitations to get mad, such as missed appointments, people getting snappy with you, even an empty coffee pot in the break room. But how many of those invitations do you really want to accept? It's important to sift through those anger invitations carefully. Saying "Yes, thanks" to too many anger invitations will mean you end up at a lot of anger parties, many of which will distract you and your coworkers from your business. Also, you'll soon get the label of "hothead" if you get into frequent disputes with your coworkers. That label could hurt you a lot in terms of raises, promotions, etc. You'll need to be quite selective. Remember that "smart fish don't bite," and keep out of useless fights and arguments.

Why Can't I Just Let Off a Little Steam?

First of all, chances are that your concept of "little" is part of the problem. What exactly do you mean when you use that term? Many people who have learned to be yellers and throwers don't realize how loud they get and how far they throw. You may be scaring your coworkers with your King Kong act.

But here's something even more important to think about. Research has shown repeatedly that the more you ventilate your anger, the more angry you get. That means every time you let off that steam you're training yourself to shout and throw things more and more often (Tavris, 1989). The more steam you let off, the more you'll end up smoking. Your supposedly harmless ventilation is actually making you into an angrier human being.

One more consideration: The modern workplace rewards personal discipline. The last thing you need is to demonstrate to your coworkers and supervisors that you are a master of loss of control. That's what you're doing every time you indulge in the luxury of a shout, scream, or throw. Do you really want to do that?

When Is Anger Justified?

There are two versions of this answer, one practical and the other moral.

The practical version emphasizes the effects of the other person's behavior upon you. Your anger is justified only when another's inappropriate actions directly and immediately hinder your job performance. One example would be that your coworker forgets to return an important file that you urgently need and is currently locked in his office. Note that the actual intent of the other person is not the issue. It doesn't matter whether or not he left the file in his office on purpose. You have the right to get angry simply because his behavior has negatively affected you. Your anger is serving its signal function here by telling you that something is definitely wrong and needs your attention and energy. Using this criterion helps people from getting mad when another person's behavior is merely bothersome or annoying but doesn't actually affect their job performance.

The moral answer is a little different. The idea here is that anger is only justified when another worker has intentionally done something damaging to you such as locking the files in his office just to keep you from doing your job. Since people don't usually sit around dreaming up ways to screw up their coworkers, it's unlikely that you can justify getting angry very often if you adopt the moral perspective on anger.

There is one more moral situation that may justify anger. Sometimes coworkers do things that deeply violate a person's values. Perhaps, for example, you are working on a plumbing crew and you watch your boss pretend to be working on something in order to cheat an old woman out of a lot of money. True, your boss isn't harming you, but he is harming someone else. Then, too, your anger is indeed justified.

What's Good About Anger in the Workplace?

Anger is a natural emotion that has several valuable uses. Perhaps the most important is that it tells someone that something is seriously wrong and needs immediate attention. It's a signal that can only be ignored at the risk of things getting even worse. Since anger is also an energizer, it helps people both recognize that there is a problem and become aroused enough to take action about it. Anger stimulates productive action.

Your anger also warns others to be careful, at least if you show your anger in a nonviolent way (verbally or nonverbally). Your coworkers can then either stay away until you cool down or approach you to try to help deal with the problem.

Anger increases one's awareness of self and other. In particular, it helps people notice and protect their boundaries. Sometimes getting angry is part of being able to say "no" to a coworker's unreasonable expectations or demands. Anger isn't so good with "yes," though, so people who get too angry too often frequently find themselves isolated from others and without a positive agenda for their lives.

Moral anger in the workplace can be used to defend a belief or principle. Here the worker may fight not for personal gain but to make the workplace a more honest, more caring, or more committed organization.

Finally, anger that is expressed appropriately may improve worker relationships and organizational productivity. The idea here is to tell people what's wrong, deal with the conflict, resolve your concerns, and get back to business. When this process is followed, workers learn that well-expressed anger helps clear up problems and mends hurt feelings.

How Is My Anger Dangerous to My Health?

Redford and Virginia Williams write that people with chronic hostility often develop significant heart problems that result in unnecessarily early death. They also note that hostility creates special problems at work, especially for managers, because "the hostile person's abrasive, aggressive personality style sabotages the very loyalty and commitment that subordinates must have if the work goals are to be met" (1994). They cite research indicating that anger characteristically increases blood pressure for hostile men. Hostile men also develop more difficulties with greater adrenaline flow and higher cholesterol secretion—a combination increasing the likelihood that they will build up excessive amounts of plaque in their arteries and thus be candidates for arteriosclerosis. Yes, chronic anger can be dangerous to your health.

But impulsive bursts of anger may endanger your health for other reasons. Nobody knows how many industrial accidents result from someone's sudden rage but the number certainly must be significant. Imagine a car mechanic getting frustrated under the hood and in a moment of rage slamming his fist on the floor or wall hard enough to break a bone. There's also the risk that a worker's anger can lead to injurious physical fights.

The point is that two sets of people can be harmed by your anger: everybody else and you. You may want to start becoming less angry for pure self-interest, so that you can stay alive and healthy longer.

Why Can't I Stop Getting Angry?

It's one thing to want to get less angry and another to do so. People can run into difficulty quitting for many reasons. These include a desire to stay in *control* of others ("Sure, I'd like to be less angry, but that's the best way to get what I want around here"); *poor communication skills* ("I try to tell people what I want but I never can get through to them. That's when I get frustrated and really blow up"); *habit* ("I keep falling back into anger just like it's a bad habit. Giving up smoking was easier than this"); *distorted thinking patterns* ("I have a hard time seeing any good in anybody") and *enjoyment of the anger feeling* ("I get a rush when I get really mad. It's kind of a high").

Depression, chronic physical illness and some cognitive disorders like paranoia may also contribute heavily to a worker's inability to quit being angry. So can the existence of family or relationship problems that eat away at a person's self-esteem and sense of hope.

You might need help if you've really been trying hard to be less angry and haven't succeeded so far. Try seeing your company's Employee Assistance program representative, a counselor or psychologist who specializes in anger management, or perhaps a doctor who can test you for various physical and emotional difficulties.

Are There Any Medicines to Help Me with My Anger?

At the time of this writing there is no single pill designed primarily for the purpose of containing anger. One reason for this is because the sources of anger are so varied that no single medicine could tackle them all. However, research is being conducted that keeps shedding more light on how the same kind of serotonin deficiencies that lead to depression and alcoholism also contribute to some forms of anger. The end product of that research could be the development of a specific anti-anger drug.

Until then, each angry person must be treated on a case-by-case basis. If an underlying physical cause is indeed discovered then medications for that condition may also help with anger. Antidepressants, for instance, often work dramatically to lessen the depressed worker's irrational anger. Tegretol, an anticonvulsant, is also used on occasion, along with a raft of medications that include antipsychotics, beta blockers like propanolol, anti-anxiety medicines, and mood stabilizers like lithium.

The best thing for you to do if you believe your anger may be caused by a medical condition is to see a physician or psychiatrist for a thorough evaluation.

How Can I Make a Committment to Be Less Angry?

A good place to start is with a promise to yourself to stay calm for one whole day. In fact, I strongly suggest you use the form below:

The Promise

I, _____,
promise to stay calm for twenty-four hours, beginning at
_____ a.m./p.m. on _____ (day),
_____ (year).
Your signature _____

Witness _____

Why a formal promise? Because it reminds you this is very serious business. Quitting being excessively angry is something that takes a strong and unequivocal commitment. As they say in Alcoholics Anonymous, "Half measures avail us nothing." Why a witness? Because that will increase your commitment level by making your promise something that is shared and supported by others.

There are several other ways you can prepare to change your behavior. One is to tell your coworkers about your goal. Ask your best friends at work for support. Perhaps one of them will be willing to remind you about your pledge if you seem to be slipping. It will also be very helpful for you to review your reasons for wanting to be less angry, both external ones (like the fear of being canned) and internal ones (such as wanting finally to feel less defensive or unhappy). Don't let yourself bargain or compromise, either. No "I'll be less angry if they're nice to me" stuff. That kind of thinking just sets you up for failure the first time someone at work does something you don't like. Finally, plan ahead. Is there a particularly difficult meeting today? Do you have to do some task you dislike? Think through what might get you frustrated and figure out what you could do to stay calm.

Are There Different Issues for a Woman Who's Angry at Work?

This question refers to what might be called "the 'bitch' factor": because a woman's anger is less societally accepted, she is often labeled a "bitch" for normal expressions of anger or annoyance. So, although women probably get just as angry as men at work, they may be penalized more for their anger. While men's anger is tolerated because men are supposedly naturally aggressive, women's anger is often perceived as weird and unfeminine. Certainly there is no term in the English language for men that implies a negative judgment of someone who is angry as does the word "bitch."

It's also true that some people cannot distinguish between a strong woman and an angry one. They label a woman's appropriate acts of assertiveness as signs she is pushy and aggressive, even though that woman is merely asserting her thoughts and rights while not damaging anyone else. Women within organizations dominated by people with such beliefs are caught in a difficult situation—they are perceived by others either as nice or as strong but never as both.

Given this dilemma, some women opt for niceness so they can gain approval from their coworkers; others choose strength even though that means they will be isolated and disliked. Hopefully this unnecessary problem is gradually being eliminated as more men and women realize that a woman can be both strong and nice at the same time.

So, societal prejudices against women may be part of the problem if you are accused of being too angry or hostile at work. But be careful about dismissing other workers' concerns or complaints with this explanation. It's still critical that you take a good look at yourself. Could there be a nugget of truth in these accusations? Do you have some anger issues that would need your attention even if you were working in a totally enlightened atmosphere?

How Can I Slow Down My Temper?

You'd think workers with anger problems would know a lot about how their anger builds up to a boil. But often they don't. Their anger seems to just explode on them because they don't attend to the signs of accelerating anger inside them.

The way to learn about these cues is to ask yourself the following questions:

- What did I think *right before* I blew up last time?

- What did I say?

- What did I do?

- What physical sensations did I have (literally, what did I feel)?

The answers to these questions provide warning beacons announcing that you're heading quickly into dangerous territory. Perhaps last time you blew up you thought "I can't take this anymore," you said to your coworker that he better back off right now, or you began pacing around as your stomach tightened up. So next time you think/say/do/feel any of these things, you'll know you are about to blow. Take an immediate time-out. Cool down. Get safe.

Keep working at recognizing how your anger builds up. You'll begin noticing earlier and earlier the signs that will help you control your anger more quickly and effectively.

How Can I Accept Criticism Better?

Show me someone who says they like criticism and I'll show you a liar. The narcissist in each of us much prefers total admiration. "Why, Ginnie, you're the best worker we've ever had around here. Please accept this huge raise, a promotion, and our eternal gratitude." Sadly, the world sometimes doesn't appreciate us as much as we'd prefer. Sometimes our coworkers and supervisors even dare to make suggestions or criticize us. That's when we need to find the courage to take in their criticism without lashing back at them ("Oh yeah? What do you know about this anyhow. Keep your nose out of my business") or silently stewing.

The best way to handle criticism is to adopt an accepting attitude centering on the idea that people make these suggestions and comments for the sake of the greater good, not simply to bother you. The goal at work, after all, is to produce the best product possible, whether that results in machines, sales, or ideas. Furthermore, there's almost always something worth considering in other people's approaches to a problem. It's important to get past ego concerns to consider their ideas seriously.

You may be too thin-skinned—oversensitive to criticism. This can be a sign of low self-esteem. You may feel deep inside that you're really not good enough, a sure sign of shame that often leads to a fear others will judge you as severely as you do. If so, you might want to find out what that's all about by going to counseling or reading about shame and self-esteem on your own. Until you deal with your low self-esteem, you will continue to have difficulty listening to other's criticisms without thinking they are completely condemning you.

What If I'm Just Being Funny?

Probably every joke, sarcastic remark, and act of horseplay has a little anger in it. But some workers' jokes and other attempts at humor are just plain too aggressive. That's when their colleagues react negatively.

The best question to ask here is who is the butt of your jokes? If the answer is you yourself, then there should be no problem. A joke like that usually begins with "You know what I just did? I stapled my papers to my tie," or, "I went to work an hour early only to find out it was Saturday," and so on.

How often, though, do your jokes follow the format "You know what _____ just did? She ..." Now one of your coworkers has become the butt of your humor. Perhaps you can get away with this once in a while but probably not for long. Soon your coworkers will realize that your so-called humor is really an excuse to call them names and make fun of them. Your jokes then become a sign of ill will that breeds resentment.

My suggestion here is quite simple: Always laugh *at* yourself and *with* others, not the other way around.

How Can I Be Less Critical of Others?

The first step in becoming less critical is to learn what you gain from your behavior. Take a good, honest look at the following statements to see how many of them help explain why you keep finding fault in others. Put a check before those that apply:

Being critical of you ...

_____ helps me feel superior/dominant

_____ validates my way of doing things by invalidating yours

_____ protects me against your criticism by striking first

_____ helps me avoid noticing my own imperfections

_____ keeps me in control by making you feel weak, dumb, or bad

_____ is just what I do to myself—I'm also very self-critical

_____ keeps you from getting to know me very well

_____ is my way of trying to help you—whether you need it or not

_____ feels good—it's fun to put people down

_____ protects my image, because what you do reflects upon me

_____ helps me feel noticed by making people pay attention to me

_____ helps me feel strong by making people afraid of me

It takes personal fortitude to admit you have some of these reasons for being critical. But that's the best way to start dealing with your habit of criticism.

The second step is to make a choice to refrain from criticism. That means holding your tongue on the many occasions you could find fault with others. Keep your eyes on your own work unless and until someone else's actions directly affect your job. Keep asking yourself, "Does it really matter if they do that job their way or my way?" Usually you'll find that their way is at least good enough to get the job done, even if it isn't quite as perfect as your plan.

The third step is to get your needs met in a more positive manner—by substituting praise for criticism. Begin looking for and remarking on what your coworkers are doing right and well instead of wrong and bad. You'll soon discover that you're appreciated a lot more. Surprisingly, you'll probably also notice that other people are doing a little better work around you. That's because your praise is a far better motivator than your criticism ever could be.

How Can I Leave Work Stress and Anger at Work?

Home is supposed to be the place you can let down your hair and really be yourself. But that doesn't give anybody in the family the right to make it the place they can be miserable and make everybody else feel awful, too. Home is definitely not a dump where you can throw the entire workday's garbage.

It's often helpful to give yourself a little transition time between home after work. I'm not talking about stopping by the local pub for a couple hours, though. What I suggest is that you take fifteen minutes to half an hour once you get home quietly reading the paper, exercising, meditating, or just plain relaxing before turning your attention to your spouse and family. The goal of this transition period is to clear your mind from all those workplace frustrations. You'll have to explain why you're doing this to your family, of course, but they will probably go along with this "decompression" time if you can really feel more peaceful when you join them afterwards.

But are you really sure you can't deal with your concerns at work before you go home? You may be familiar with the common saying about relationships, "Don't go to bed mad." Perhaps a workplace equivalent would be helpful, something like "Don't go home from work mad." This would imply that you're making every effort to clear up any problems before the end of the day. Remembering this idea will help break the habit of stuffing your anger at work and then hauling it home.

Will Minimizing My Anger Decrease My Power at Work?

Many people fear that letting go of their anger at work will turn them into "wimps." Wimps are passive people who never stand up for themselves even when they're treated very badly. To be wimpy is to be weak, scared, timid, and ineffectual. Just by asking this question you are indicating how important it is for you to see yourself (and be seen by others) as strong, courageous, and effective. And that's exactly what assertiveness is all about. Assertive workers are able to handle difficult situations by clearly telling others what they think, feel, want, and need.

The difference between assertive and aggressive behavior is that aggressors attack others with their words and actions in order to get what they want, while assertive people address others in the hope of finding mutually beneficial solutions to conflicts. Aggressors are mostly interested in what's good for them. Assertive workers try to find out what's good for everybody.

The wimp is nice but weak. The aggressor is strong but mean. By practicing assertiveness, you can learn to be strong without getting mean.

What Are the Rules for Fair Fighting?

Here's a list of fair fighting rules originally printed in my book, *Angry All the Time*. Although intended originally for the family, they apply equally well to work conflict.

Fair Fighting Rules

Do	Don't
tell people what you feel	make fun of others
stick to one issue at a time	hit, push, shove, hold, or threaten to do so
sit down and talk	stand up and yell
listen	make faces
focus on the specific behavior you want	attack the other's personality
make regular eye contact (but don't glare)	name call
be flexible—be willing to change your mind	get stuck in the past
breathe calmly, stay relaxed	run away from the issue
be open to negotiation and compromise	say "forget it," "tough," "I don't care," "so what," or anything that ignores the other's concerns
be responsible for everything you say	have to get the last word in
focus on solutions, not victories or defeats	interrupt
take time-outs as needed	say "always" or "never" or other generalizations

These fair-fighting rules must be practiced and used. So don't just glance at them. Make a copy and put it in your purse or wallet. Take it out and read it before you start talking with someone about a conflict. Also, this list is for you. It's great if others abide by the rules as well, but don't let their behavior determine yours. Stick to the rules regardless of what others do, and you'll feel considerably better about yourself.

How Can I Take a Time-Out When I Can't Physically Leave?

Actually there are many times when a time-out is impractical or impossible—you may be driving in a truck with the person you're angry with, your boss may be lecturing you, or you have responsibilities that keep you firmly planted in your chair. You're starting to fume, you'd like to get away, and you can't.

That's when you need to take an *inner time-out*. Only you know you're doing this because it happens inside you. Concentrate on taking one deep breath at a time. Tell yourself you're not going to let the other person make you lose control. Put up an inner wall that filters out most of that person's words. Listen just enough to hear anything important and tune out the rest.

Taking an inner time-out is not the same as ignoring someone. You're doing two things more when you take an inner time-out. First, you are maintaining responsibility for your behavior by not letting the other person pull the trigger on your emotions. Second, you're practicing self-control by taking those deep breaths, actually proving to yourself you can stay calm no matter what is happening around you.

Could I Be Covering Up My Real Feelings with Anger?

Anger can be what's called a "cover emotion." That means you're using anger to hide your other feelings from yourself as well as your coworkers. People do that because once they've developed the habit of anger it's easier to get mad than to deal with any other feeling. Anger becomes an old pal you always hang out with while your other emotions seem like strangers. Sadness, joy, fear, and all your other emotions may be far more scary for you to handle than anger because anger is the feeling you are most familiar with. This creates a vicious downhill spiral: the more you hide your other feelings from yourself the less chance you have to learn how to deal with them; the less chance to deal with them the more you get afraid of them; the more afraid of them the more you hide them from yourself.

Think of your anger as if it were a blanket. That blanket is your emotional cover. The rest of your feelings are tucked under, but you'll never get to know what they are until you take off the blanket. Try taking a peek under the cover by asking yourself this question: "If I weren't getting angry now, what other emotions would I let myself feel?"

But the feelings that you cover with anger aren't necessarily your *only* feelings or your true feelings. Don't discount your anger by saying all it's doing is hiding the rest, because your other emotions may be no more real than your anger. You have to be honest with yourself here by deciding if your anger is mostly an act designed to conceal your real feelings or if your anger simply comes on so strong the others get pushed into the background. In either case, however, keep open to the probability that there may be more feelings going on inside you than you realize, and that you may be ignoring those other feelings when you pay attention only to your anger.

Why Do My Coworkers Think I'm Angry When I'm Not?

Your face may be fooling them. Many people simply look angry when all they're doing is concentrating on their work. That's because the facial cues for anger include narrowed eyes, furrowed eyebrows, and tightened lips. Some individuals naturally scrunch up their faces when they're angry *and* when concentrating. That might confuse your coworkers enough to mistake one for the other.

On the other hand, maybe you actually *are* angry some of the time without realizing it, and that anger is showing up in your face. If that's the case, it's like you're walking around advertising your anger to everybody but yourself. Perhaps you'd better begin noticing more what's going on up there. If your face says you're mad, but your mind says you're not, there's obviously an internal communication breakdown you'd better attend to quickly. So, either relax your face to make it consistent with your mind, or find out why your face is looking so grumpy.

How Can I Tolerate a Particularly Irritating Person?

Sometimes it seems like the gods of work have diabolically presented you with your very own, special nemesis, an individual seemingly put on this earth with the sole purpose of bothering you. Almost everything that person does is annoying: their voice, the way they walk, their stupid ideas, and so on. It feels like fingernails grating against the blackboard every time you have to meet with them. There's even a good chance that this coworker reminds you all too well of someone in your past who you had to get away from, such as a parent, ex-partner, or a bad boss. It's almost like that person has reappeared to haunt you, in a new body.

The single most important thing to do if you are facing such a nemesis is to separate that person from your past. You have to remind yourself frequently that "No, he's not Fred. He's Joe. True, he does happen to say some of the same things Fred did, but he's not Fred. He's Joe." Then make yourself notice some of the things Joe does differently from Fred to emphasize the dissimilarities between them.

You also might want to take a quick projection test here. Ask yourself this question: "Is that person I dislike so much doing things I wish I could do myself but don't dare?" One example would be that your nemesis can be weak and whiny while you are stuck trying to be strong and independent. You feel contemptuous about their neediness but secretly wish people would notice that sometimes you could use a little help and comfort too. It's really easy to despise coworkers who do just what you've forced yourself not to do. Hating them covers up your envy. Your anger may be telling you that you have some unmet needs at work, which perhaps could be met, if you allowed yourself to acknowledge them.

The third thing to do is to "de-monsterize" your coworker. No, he or she isn't the personification of evil—just another human being who happens to do things very differently than you. Since you probably can't change that person, it would be in your best interest to accept reality. Besides, dealing with people you don't like much is an inevitable part of most work environments. Fortunately, there's no rule that says you have to like every one of your coworkers. So try to figure out why this particular person bugs you so much, notice your own wants and needs, keep your focus on getting the job done, and accept the inevitable.

Will I Take This Anger to My Next Job?

"Geographic flight" is the term used in Alcoholics Anonymous when someone leaves one location for another to avoid dealing with their drinking problem. Chronically angry persons often do the same, becoming disgruntled at one job, quitting in a huff or getting fired, going to another only to suffer the same result, and continually repeating the process. So, one way to answer your question is for you to take a good long look at both your work and personal histories. Specifically: Does your family talk about how difficult you were to raise? Were you a hothead as a teenager, often defying your parents or school authorities? Did you ever get suspended or expelled from school for fighting, disobedience, or absenteeism (which is a passive form of defiance)? Have you had problems at work before, either on your current job or in previous employment? Have you ever been warned or disciplined because of anger-related behavior before this job? Have you been told repeatedly that you have a bad attitude or an anger problem? Have you had bouts of depression or other physical or emotional problems in the past (if so, could that be the problem now?). Finally, do your longtime friends, partner, or children ever tell you to cool down, ease up, or not get so angry? If the answer to one or more or these questions is "yes," then you may very well take your anger with you to your next job. Before resigning, you may want to take a good look at yourself and take the time to work on your anger issues. Then, if unfixable concerns remain you'll be able to leave with more confidence in yourself.

Could My Recent Drinking and Drugging Be Related to My Work Anger?

A lot of workers stop at the tavern on the way home for a couple of beers. That's not necessarily a problem, unless those couple become a few and the few become many. But sometimes those workers head into the bar angry, tense, and bothered. Work didn't go well. They need to unwind. Magically, alcohol or drugs work their wonders and the worker feels more relaxed. Soon, they're thinking that drinking or drugging is the *only* way they can relax, and that's when they cross the line from social to problem drinking. It's a small step from there to true addiction, especially if one's drinking or drugging causes that person even more work problems (increased irritability, coming back from lunch hour stoned, and so on).

You'll need to get honest with yourself if you're going in this direction. Most critically, you must quit using work tension as an excuse to drink or get high. Frustration, after all, is part of life. Instead of trying to get rid of that tension by getting drunk or high you'll be far better off by directly addressing the problems as they arise at work. All you're doing right now is running away from these concerns instead of dealing with them. That simply means that your problems will still be there after you sober up or come down from that high.

You may need to seriously consider getting an alcohol/drug assessment from a local counselor or doctor. You could very well need help quitting if you've been trying to handle your anger through alcohol and drugs for a while.

Remember this: It's not that alcohol and drugs don't work, at least for a while, to relieve your anger. The problem is that they work too well—so well in fact that you can easily get hooked on them.

How Can I Avoid Getting Sucked into Others' Anger?

Workers' fights tend to expand quickly to encompass everybody in a unit, work crew, or entire organization. It's hard to avoid first being part of the audience and then being expected to take sides. Since it's a whole lot easier to get into these battles than out, it's certainly in your best interest to stay clear of them whenever possible. You will need to make a definite, conscious decision not to get swept up in these fights. Then you'll need to act firmly to convey that message to your colleagues.

Here are a few tips on what to do and say in these situations:

1. Politely decline invitations to take sides ("Holly, I know you want me to get involved here, but I think the issues are between you and Urna. I think you should talk to her about it").

2. Limit your willingness to be part of the audience ("Max, let's talk about something else. All this anger is getting me down").

3. Stay away from "complaint centers," where people congregate to complain about the company or specific individuals. This might imply taking a walk at break time instead of sitting with the old gang, if that group is habitually angry.

4. Remember that there are always two sides to every story. It's more tempting to get angry when you're only hearing one of those sides.

5. Stick with your decision even in the face of guilt trips and accusations of disloyalty as well as your own fears of being rejected. Keep telling yourself that it's not worth your while to get sucked into all that anger, no matter what people say about you.

How Can I Tell My Friend That They Have an Anger Problem?

Do you dare? Will your friend chop off your head when you approach with your concerns? Will you still be friends, or will you have become that person's mortal enemy? There's no doubt that trying to tell anyone, much less a friend, that they have an anger problem is risky. But who is going to say anything if you won't? Wouldn't you want your friend to let you know about something you were doing that was causing a lot of problems? So I suggest you speak up, unless you know for a fact that the result will be disastrous.

Let's look at the when, where, and how of this action.

- **When?** When that person is *not* angry or upset. He or she will be far less defensive then, and you'll be less likely to get caught up in the latest feud.

- **Where?** At work, on their turf, such as in their office or work area. People feel safer in their own space and therefore more likely to listen.

- **How?** Face to face. Sitting down. Speaking quietly. Giving recent and specific examples about how your friend's anger is affecting his or her performance, mood, and overall happiness. Making it clear that it's that person's choice as to how to use this information and that you'll still be their friend whatever they choose to do with it. Not getting hooked into arguing or trying to prove your point. Speaking from your heart to theirs. Expecting nothing except to be heard.

Should I Resign If My Workplace Is Too Angry?

There's no doubt that working in an angry, hostile company can be a miserable experience. It's no fun to see people so unnecessarily hurting each other. Even if you don't get caught up personally in the attacks, the sheer negativity is depressing. That's when all the joys and challenges of work are likely to be lost. Who wouldn't want to get away from that kind of situation?

However, before disrupting your life by quitting, ask yourself if there's anything you could do in your organization to help your coworkers be less angry with each other. Sometimes it's as simple as bringing up the problem at a general meeting or with your work associates. They may be just as sick of the bickering as you are and ready to make some changes.

Do you have any hope that things can change for the better? If so, maybe you could stick around for a while to help bring about some positive changes. If not, then it's time to print up your résumé and start looking around.

In general, too much anger at work destroys morale, lowers efficiency, and causes a variety of other troubles. But the problem is much more immediate if you personally have an anger problem at work. It's best to be honest with yourself if you do. You'll have to take personal responsibility for your behavior instead of blaming others. This can be difficult, but the payoff is feeling better at work and taking less stress home at the end of the day.

If you have identified yourself as an angry worker, you'll want to look carefully at the specific tools and techniques I offered earlier in the book. However, anger management goes beyond skill development. Letting go of excessive anger is also a journey of the heart, as I'll discuss in the next chapter.

7

Beyond Technique: A Journey of Head and Heart

Communication Techniques Aren't Enough

I once worked with an excellent psychologist who often saw couples for marital therapy. One day I asked him what communications techniques, such as the use of "I" statements or fair-fighting rules, he recommended the most. His answer was instructive. He told me that these communication techniques were helpful to some couples, but that they often proved insufficient. "What good are they," he asked me, "when the people just use them to attack each other?" He went on to say that, in his experience, the couples who saved their marriages were those who could find something deep inside themselves that allowed them to take personal responsibility for their part in the problem, to accept their partners as separate and unique persons, and to forgive each other for the damages, intended and unintended, they had each done. Good mechanics alone simply wasn't enough. The people who utilized these techniques must also possess good hearts for the techniques to work well. My experience with anger management at work is the same. Yes, I can easily teach workers the techniques of anger and conflict prevention, containment, and resolution. And no, those techniques alone simply don't improve the situation much.

The problem is that workplace conflict affects people's core sense of hope. The longer conflict continues, the greater its intensity, the more damage it does, the less workers believe that anything good can happen. Finally, people come to a tipping point, where the balance between optimism and pessimism tilts way over toward pessimism. Something awful happens inside them then: they give up both the belief that they can help resolve the problems and that the troubles will ever cease. That's when workers may begin to suffer two maladies of the soul. First they become dispirited: they lose energy, sinking into an attitude of "I'm just coming to work to get a paycheck." Second, they become mean-spirited: their formerly positive energy transforms into cynicism, negativity, criticism, and hostility.

Fortunately, this journey into despair is not inevitable. Many workers maintain a sense of hope even in difficult circumstances. They seem to have a powerful belief system inside them that helps them keep seeking positive resolutions even in the face of others' doubts and disparagements. Their optimism is resilient as well. They learn from their defeats rather than being totally discouraged by them. They refuse to relinquish their core convictions that the workplace can be a safe and mutually respectful organization.

These workers are on a journey of head and heart. They use their heads to think through their problems and conflicts, doing everything they can to discover effective ways to prevent useless conflicts, lessen the intensity of their anger, and find acceptable solutions to their real conflicts. They use their hearts to stay hopeful and to seek the common goodness in human beings which serves as the cornerstone for mutual caring and respect.

Eight Beliefs That Help You Stay on the Journey

A powerful set of interwoven beliefs help people stay hopeful while undertaking this journey of head and heart. Eight beliefs serve to summarize this system:

1. The belief that most people want to work together in peace

2. The belief that people have a responsibility to practice mutuality and cooperation in the workplace

3. The belief that, even during conflict, people can choose to respect each other's inherent dignity

4. The belief that, at the deepest level of existence, there are no enemies, that we are all on the same side despite the appearance of opposition, and that when people search hard enough they can and will discover common ground and mutual connection

5. The belief that people can always draw upon their reservoirs of inner strength during conflicts to discover mutually beneficial solutions

6. The belief that everyone can emerge from conflict stronger, more compassionate, and more deeply connected, as long as that conflict is handled well

7. The belief that people can find within them the ability to handle their anger with moderation so that an interpersonal dialogue can be maintained

8. The belief that people can forgive, let go of the past, and move forward together after a painful conflict.

Most People Want to Work Together in Peace

This belief is deceptively simple in its appearance. Of course, it's easy to think that people want to work together in peace. Who wouldn't? This statement sounds very much like a harmless platitude, the kind of naïve statement that only lasts until the first real controversy. That's when people drop their gloves and come out swinging. Once people's adrenaline starts pumping, you can forget about working together in peace. But that moment of instant mutual antagonism is just the time that people most need to deeply and profoundly believe that their coworkers really do want to work together in peace. It's exactly when one's body says "Fight!" that one's mind must decline the invitation.

The word "cooperate" is derived from a Latin word meaning "to work with." People not only must work with each other, they mostly want to. Why else do so many people complain about isolated working conditions in which contacts are infrequent? Why doesn't everybody seek to work the graveyard shift? Why does the word "loner" conjure up a feeling of sadness for someone who is missing out on the meaningful connections that work offers? What I'm saying is that fruitful cooperation is the norm for the human race, not the exception. Indeed, one of the reasons people pay so much attention to anger and conflict is that these conditions threaten to break the important bonds that make work a positive experience. It's in most people's best interest to resolve conflicts as quickly as possible. And that's why the proposition that people want to work together in peace is far more than a platitude. Rather, it's a powerful, active, driving force. People don't just passively hope they can work together without excessive conflict. They do everything they can to make that happen.

Cooperation in the Workplace Is Every Worker's Responsibility

Anybody watching one kid bop another on the head with a toy and then turn away with complete disinterest as the victim begins to cry knows that there is nothing automatic about cooperative behavior. If, as I suggest above, the desire to work together in harmony is deeply ingrained in the human psyche, the *practice* of cooperative work is seldom easy or automatic. Cooperation is a fairly high-level human skill. Children need to be taught how to use their natural desire to bond so they can get beyond the parallel play stage of early childhood. That is primarily the job of parents and teachers. These people often use pretend work situations to prepare their charges for the real world. By simulating the conditions of a workplace they're encouraging their children to play the great game called "mutuality" or "cooperation." Hopefully, by the time we reach adulthood, most of us will have had many opportunities to practice and even master that gentle art.

While learning how to cooperate employs many general rules (take turns, share and share alike, there is no "I" in the word "team," etc.), it's also true that each work situation is unique. That means, for example, the specifics of cooperative behavior may be quite different on the intake unit of a social services department than in the sales room of a shoe factory. It's our responsibility as adult members of a work organization to discover and utilize these situation-specific rules. Each of us must learn the "how" of cooperation in our particular endeavors.

But why is this a responsibility? Because mutual cooperation is by no means a luxury or something kind of nice to have around. These days, working together is a necessary condition of modern employment. For example, take the billing clerk in an electrical installation firm. That person simply can't do their job without everybody else's cooperative participation. Unnecessary anger and useless conflict only mess up the fragile systems that are the basis of modern organization.

Personal responsibility goes beyond simply understanding a set of rules or guidelines. It means that each member of a work organization can and should help create and maintain a safe work climate for everyone. By "safe" I refer both to physical safety and to verbal assault.

People Can Choose to Respect Others' Inherent Dignity

Conflict can be a nasty business. All too often, conflicts spiral out of control. People start attacking each other with every weapon in their possession, striving to shame and humiliate each other. Original concerns get left behind, as those who disagree slide from discussing real issues to demeaning each other's personality. Everybody gets hurt in these battles and the damage is often difficult to undo. Although these personality attacks are totally unnecessary, they are hard to resist because they give people moments of intense satisfaction: "Aha, now I've got that s.o.b. That will show people they'd better not mess with me."

I believe that it takes more courage *not* to attack others this way during conflict than to attack. Certainly it takes more discipline. The goal here is to choose not to hurt someone else, even though you could, and even though you may very well want to. The way to refrain is to remember that winning a victory by harming someone else is disrespectful both of their dignity and yours. The bottom line is that each of us has to look ourselves in the mirror at night after work. How can we respect ourselves if, during the day, we have disrespected others? Besides, disrespectful behavior only breeds an atmosphere of anger and discord. The result is that the person who initiates personality attacks one day may very well become the victim of such assaults the next.

Choice is the key word here. People always have choices in the area of conflict, no matter how angry and upset they become. It's always possible to choose the path of respect.

There Are No Enemies

During the course of writing this book I have tried to minimize the use of combat metaphors to describe conflict situations. I did this because thinking of conflict in terms of combat metaphors tends to escalate the intensity of the conflict. Disagreements become "fights," the people we disagree with become "enemies," and the long-term situations become "wars." Combat metaphors seem utterly natural to describe conflict, however, if only because of their frequent use, historically. The very word "conflict" is actually derived from a Latin term meaning "to strike together."

The problem with utilizing combat metaphors to describe conflict is the implication that those who disagree with each other experience a fundamental division that separates them now and perhaps forever. In other words, they are on opposite sides. The unanswered question, though, is on opposite sides of what? Of a trench? A position? An argument?

It's easy to get bound up in division and separation during the passion generated by conflict. What gets lost is the quiet certainty that in deeper ways, no matter how great the conflict, human beings have much more in common than they have differences. Our underlying humanity can be ignored but cannot be denied. We are all fellow travelers along the path of life.

I'm not saying that all conflict is illusory, or that the feeling of separation because of conflict is imaginary. But it is possible and necessary to nourish the sense of mutuality even during conflict by focusing on our commonalties rather than differences. In that manner we can remember to look for that which connects all human beings despite the appearance of disconnection.

There are many possible alternative metaphors that describe conflictual situations without resorting to combat analogies. Here are a few:

- a batch of puppies squabbling for a minute, only to resettle in a clump to continue their nap

- two rivers, one fast and rocky, the other wide and slow, but both making their way to the common waters of the ocean

- two people straining to move a heavy object, one pushing and the other pulling, as they gradually achieve their goal

- an unstoppable forest fire that, even while it ignites the trees, clears the path for future growth

- a parent hearing an angered child say "I hate you" and still feeling great love for that child

- two lost souls needing each other's skills to find their way out of the forest

Perhaps you could use one of these metaphors to help you remember even during conflicts the underlying connectiveness shared by all. In that manner, you will help open the flow of energy between separation and connection rather than getting locked into separation.

You Can Discover a Mutually Beneficial Solution

There comes a time in many conflicts called the impasse. An impasse is a stuck point, a seemingly unresolvable issue that makes further progress impossible. Work conflicts frequently lead to impasses, when people throw up their hands and say they've done all they can, but they can't get anywhere. That's when they often blast the other parties in the conflict, basically saying that everything could be settled quickly if it weren't for the other parties' obstinancy. The fact that both sides feel the same way about the other indicates that perhaps everybody is slightly misunderstanding the situation. It would be better to recognize that impasses are simply a normal part of the negotiating experience. Indeed, impasses occur because people believe strongly in their ideas. The only way to completely avoid impasses is not to care about any goal, process, or idea enough to fight for it.

People get through these stuck points by reaching inside a little deeper to discover mutually beneficial solutions. That often involves rethinking one's entire viewpoint, becoming more flexible, focusing upon interests instead of positions, and listening more attentively to the other parties' wants and needs. An openness to creative possibility also helps greatly—the willingness to accept new ways to resolve problems. In these ways, many workers have discovered that impasses are the seeds for cooperative problem solving.

It takes time and effort to find these collaborative solutions. Most of all, it takes the courage to reach beyond the obvious—an apparently deadlocked conflict—to find ways to get everyone back to working together.

A Well-Handled Conflict Can Strengthen Connections

Conflict, in itself, is a neutral event—neither something to be fervently desired nor desperately avoided. Well handled, conflict can be a force that leads to personal and organizational growth. Poorly handled, conflict diminishes the self and the group. That is simple reality. However, few people have this essentially objective, nonemotional perspective on conflict. Many persons have an essentially negative view of conflict usually based upon the times that they've been hurt in conflictual situations. Others, probably fewer in number, look forward to conflict because of the benefits they perceive will emerge during conflict. This latter belief, that the results of conflict will most likely be beneficial, increases the likelihood for the person who holds it that indeed some good will come to them during conflict.

The benefits from well-handled conflict go well past merely settling a particular dispute quickly. Other gains include attending to self ("I got what I needed"), improvements in self-esteem ("I'm a good person"), an increased sense of efficacy ("I'm capable and competent"), an enlarged sense of compassion ("I care about others as well as myself"), and a deeper sense of interpersonal connection ("We've done this together").

Conflict management is a skill. It takes experience, knowledge, and wisdom for conflict to be beneficial. But, when it does work, conflict can enrich your personal and interpersonal spheres. Certainly, the work group that learns how to deal with their disagreements positively will succeed in their goals far better than either the group that avoids and evades conflict or the group that cannot resolve their disputes.

People Can Moderate Their Anger to Achieve an Open Dialogue

The topic of moderation was mentioned in the previous chapter on anger reduction and containment. My observation was that people can become so angry that they can no longer really talk *with* each other because they are basically shouting *at* each other instead. The emotion of anger helps energize people enough to begin conversations. When that anger becomes too intense, however, shared dialogue becomes impossible and is replaced by monologue. Really angry people may think they're communicating with others. The fact is that they are simply talking to themselves in a really loud voice. Anger tells people that something is wrong and needs fixing.

Since most problems in modern society (and particularly at work) involve communicating with others, your anger becomes not the signal of a problem but the problem itself when it gets so strong that dialogue becomes impossible.

The important belief that helps people stay on the journey of head and heart is that they, and others, can keep their anger at moderate levels so that an interpersonal dialogue can be maintained. To accept this belief means to reject the notion that anger sometimes takes people over, leaving them helpless to do anything but rant and rave. Discarding that belief takes away the excuse that "I couldn't help what I said (or did). I just lost control."

It's certainly true that some people have shorter fuses than others. It's exactly these people who most need to adopt the belief that they can always keep their anger within moderate levels. They cannot afford the luxury of excusing their anger explosions as beyond their control, at least not if they truly wish to work better with others. But regardless of the length of any person's anger fuse, it makes sense to believe that you can contain your anger because that belief is far more empowering than thinking you cannot.

People Can Forgive and Move On

Despite your best efforts, some conflict is painful. Intentionally or unintentionally, people can get hurt and sometimes damaged badly during conflicts. Furthermore, the very people who have harmed each other may have to face each other every day, especially at work. Long after a particular dispute is resolved coworkers can carry lingering resentments about how they were treated. These resentments can make life miserable for all. The concept of "working together" seems outlandish on these occasions. "We may be working in the same place, but we're sure not working together," becomes the majority feeling.

Recovering from these tragedies begins with the belief that healing is possible rather than that the wounds suffered during these conflicts are permanent. Resenters must be willing to think in terms of forgiveness, letting go of the past, and getting on with life. None of this is easy, of course, or there wouldn't be so many books and articles on the art of forgiveness. Letting go is never easy just because people have a strong tendency to hang on to their painful memories. It's sometimes far easier to spend hours fantasizing acts of revenge against one's alleged monstrous persecutors than to discard those fantasies in favor of seeing these others again as normal human beings.

Forgiveness may not be an obligation, but it certainly is an opportunity. The primary benefactor is the *forgiver*, who can quit brooding over the past and begin enjoying the present more. The forgiven person may also benefit by a return to more normal communication patterns and relationship. Coworkers also gain when they no longer have to act as intermediaries between perpetually feuding adversaries.

A Few Last Comments

The main point of this last chapter, and indeed of this entire book, is that people *can* learn how to get along with each other at work. The way to do that is three pronged. First, it's crucial to prevent as much useless anger and harmful conflict as possible. A focus on prevention will save most workers the pain of going through many completely unnecessary conflicts. Second, conflicts that do need to be addressed must be contained and their intensity reduced so that useful dialogue can occur. Anger and conflict can easily get out of hand—and become quite harmful in the process. Third, people in the workplace must find positive solutions to their disputes through conflict resolution. The goal of a conflict is always to find a solution that maximizes everybody's gain while minimizing loss.

Achieving these goals takes time, energy, skill, and commitment. It also takes a calm body, a wise head, and a good heart. But, for all the work it sometimes takes, it is inevitably worth the effort.

References

Alberti, R. and M. Emmons. 1986. *Your Perfect Right*. San Luis Obispo, Calif.: Impact Press.

Davis, Martha, Elizabeth Robbins, and Matthew McKay. 1995. *The Relaxation and Stress Reduction Workbook*, 4th ed. Oakland, Calif.: New Harbinger Publications.

Fisher, Roger, William Ury, and Bruce Patton. 1991. *Getting to Yes: Negotiating Agreement Without Giving In*, 2nd ed. New York: Penguin Books.

Moore, Thomas. 1992. *Care of the Soul*. New York: HarperCollins.

Myers, Donald. 1994. *Violence-Free Workplace: What You Ought to Know About Contributing to a Violence-Free Workplace*. Chicago: CCH Incorporated.

Potter-Efron, Ronald. 1998. *Being, Belonging, Doing: Balancing Your Greatest Needs*. Oakland, Calif.: New Harbinger Publications.

———. 1996. *Reducing Anger in the Workplace*. Eau Claire, Mich.: First Things First.

———. 1994. *Angry All the Time: An Emergency Guide to Anger Control*. Oakland, Calif.: New Harbinger Publications.

Potter-Efron, Ronald and Patricia. 1995. *Letting Go of Anger: The Ten Most Common Anger Styles and What to Do About Them*. Oakland, Calif.: New Harbinger Publications.

———. 1989. *Letting Go of Shame*. Center City, Minn.: Hazelden/ Harper and Row.

Tavris, Carol. 1989. *Anger: The Misunderstood Emotion*, Rev. ed. New York: Touchstone.

Thomas, K. W. and R. H. Kilmann. 1974. *Thomas-Killmann Conflict Mode Instrument*. Tuxedo, New York: Xicom.

Umbreit, Mark. 1995. *Mediating Interpersonal Conflicts: A Pathway to Peace*. West Concord, Minn.: CPI Publishing.

Williams, Redford and Virginia. 1994. *Anger Kills*. New York: Harper-Perennial.

More New Harbinger Titles

ANGRY ALL THE TIME
An Emergency Guide to Anger Control
Ron Potter-Efron's emergency guide to changing anger-provoking thoughts, dealing with old resentments, asking for what you want without anger, and staying calm one day at a time.
Item ALL Paperback, $12.95

LETTING GO OF ANGER
Ron helps you recognize the ten destructive ways that people deal with anger and identify which anger styles may be undermining your personal and work relationships.
Item LET Paperback, $13.95

BEING, BELONGING, DOING
Balancing Your Three Greatest Needs
Ron's thoughtful self-discovery exercises help us reevaluate priorities and explore practical ways of keeping the crucial components of our lives integrated and in balance.
Item BBD Paperback, $10.95

BETTER BOUNDARIES
If you feel like you have trouble saying no to others, at work or at home, this book can help you establish more effective boundaries.
Item BB Paperback, $13.95

WELLNESS AT WORK
Building Resilience to Job Stress
A blueprint for taking charge of your physical and emotional health by identifying habitual patterns of negative thinking, improving communication, developing a support network, and changing the work environment to enhance wellness.
Item WORK Paperback, $17.95

Call toll-free 1-800-748-6273 to order. Have your Visa or Mastercard number ready. Or send a check for the titles you want to New Harbinger Publications, 5674 Shattuck Avenue, Oakland, CA 94609. Include $3.80 for the first book and 75¢ for each additional book to cover shipping and handling. (California residents please include appropriate sales tax.) Allow four to six weeks for delivery.

Prices subject to change without notice.

Some Other New Harbinger Self-Help Titles

Dr. Carl Robinson's Basic Baby Care, $10.95
Better Boundaries: Owning and Treasuring Your Life, $13.95
Goodbye Good Girl, $12.95
Being, Belonging, Doing, $10.95
Thoughts & Feelings, Second Edition, $18.95
Depression: How It Happens, How It's Healed, $14.95
Trust After Trauma, $13.95
The Chemotherapy & Radiation Survival Guide, Second Edition, $14.95
Heart Therapy, $13.95
Surviving Childhood Cancer, $12.95
The Headache & Neck Pain Workbook, $14.95
Perimenopause, $13.95
The Self-Forgiveness Handbook, $12.95
A Woman's Guide to Overcoming Sexual Fear and Pain, $14.95
Mind Over Malignancy, $12.95
Treating Panic Disorder and Agoraphobia, $44.95
Scarred Soul, $13.95
The Angry Heart, $14.95
Don't Take It Personally, $12.95
Becoming a Wise Parent For Your Grown Child, $12.95
Clear Your Past, Change Your Future, $13.95
Preparing for Surgery, $17.95
Coming Out Everyday, $13.95
Ten Things Every Parent Needs to Know, $12.95
The Power of Two, $12.95
It's Not OK Anymore, $13.95
The Daily Relaxer, $12.95
The Body Image Workbook, $17.95
Living with ADD, $17.95
Taking the Anxiety Out of Taking Tests, $12.95
The Taking Charge of Menopause Workbook, $17.95
Living with Angina, $12.95
Five Weeks to Healing Stress: The Wellness Option, $17.95
Choosing to Live: How to Defeat Suicide Through Cognitive Therapy, $12.95
Why Children Misbehave and What to Do About It, $14.95
When Anger Hurts Your Kids, $12.95
The Addiction Workbook, $17.95
The Mother's Survival Guide to Recovery, $12.95
The Chronic Pain Control Workbook, Second Edition, $17.95
Fibromyalgia & Chronic Myofascial Pain Syndrome, $19.95
Flying Without Fear, $13.95
Kid Cooperation: How to Stop Yelling, Nagging & Pleading and Get Kids to Cooperate, $13.95
The Stop Smoking Workbook: Your Guide to Healthy Quitting, $17.95
Conquering Carpal Tunnel Syndrome and Other Repetitive Strain Injuries, $17.95
Wellness at Work: Building Resilience for Job Stress, $17.95
An End to Panic: Breakthrough Techniques for Overcoming Panic Disorder, Second Edition, $18.95
Living Without Procrastination: How to Stop Postponing Your Life, $12.95
Goodbye Mother, Hello Woman: Reweaving the Daughter Mother Relationship, $14.95
Letting Go of Anger: The 10 Most Common Anger Styles and What to Do About Them, $12.95
Messages: The Communication Skills Workbook, Second Edition, $13.95
Coping With Chronic Fatigue Syndrome: Nine Things You Can Do, $13.95
The Anxiety & Phobia Workbook, Second Edition, $18.95
The Relaxation & Stress Reduction Workbook, Fourth Edition, $17.95
Living Without Depression & Manic Depression: A Workbook for Maintaining Mood Stability, $17.95
Coping With Schizophrenia: A Guide For Families, $15.95
Visualization for Change, Second Edition, $15.95
Postpartum Survival Guide, $13.95
Angry All the Time: An Emergency Guide to Anger Control, $12.95
Couple Skills: Making Your Relationship Work, $13.95
Self-Esteem, Second Edition, $13.95
I Can't Get Over It, A Handbook for Trauma Survivors, Second Edition, $15.95
Dying of Embarrassment: Help for Social Anxiety and Social Phobia, $13.95
The Depression Workbook: Living With Depression and Manic Depression, $17.95
Men & Grief: A Guide for Men Surviving the Death of a Loved One, $14.95
When the Bough Breaks: A Helping Guide for Parents of Sexually Abused Children, $11.95
When Once Is Not Enough: Help for Obsessive Compulsives, $13.95
The Three Minute Meditator, Third Edition, $12.95
Beyond Grief: A Guide for Recovering from the Death of a Loved One, $13.95
Hypnosis for Change: A Manual of Proven Techniques, Third Edition, $15.95
When Anger Hurts, $13.95

Call **toll free, 1-800-748-6273,** to order. Have your Visa or Mastercard number ready. Or send a check for the titles you want to New Harbinger Publications, Inc., 5674 Shattuck Ave., Oakland, CA 94609. Include $3.80 for the first book and 75¢ for each additional book, to cover shipping and handling. (California residents please include appropriate sales tax.) Allow two to five weeks for delivery.

Prices subject to change without notice.